The executive Power shall be vested in a President of the United States of America.
—Constitution of the United States
Article II, Section 1

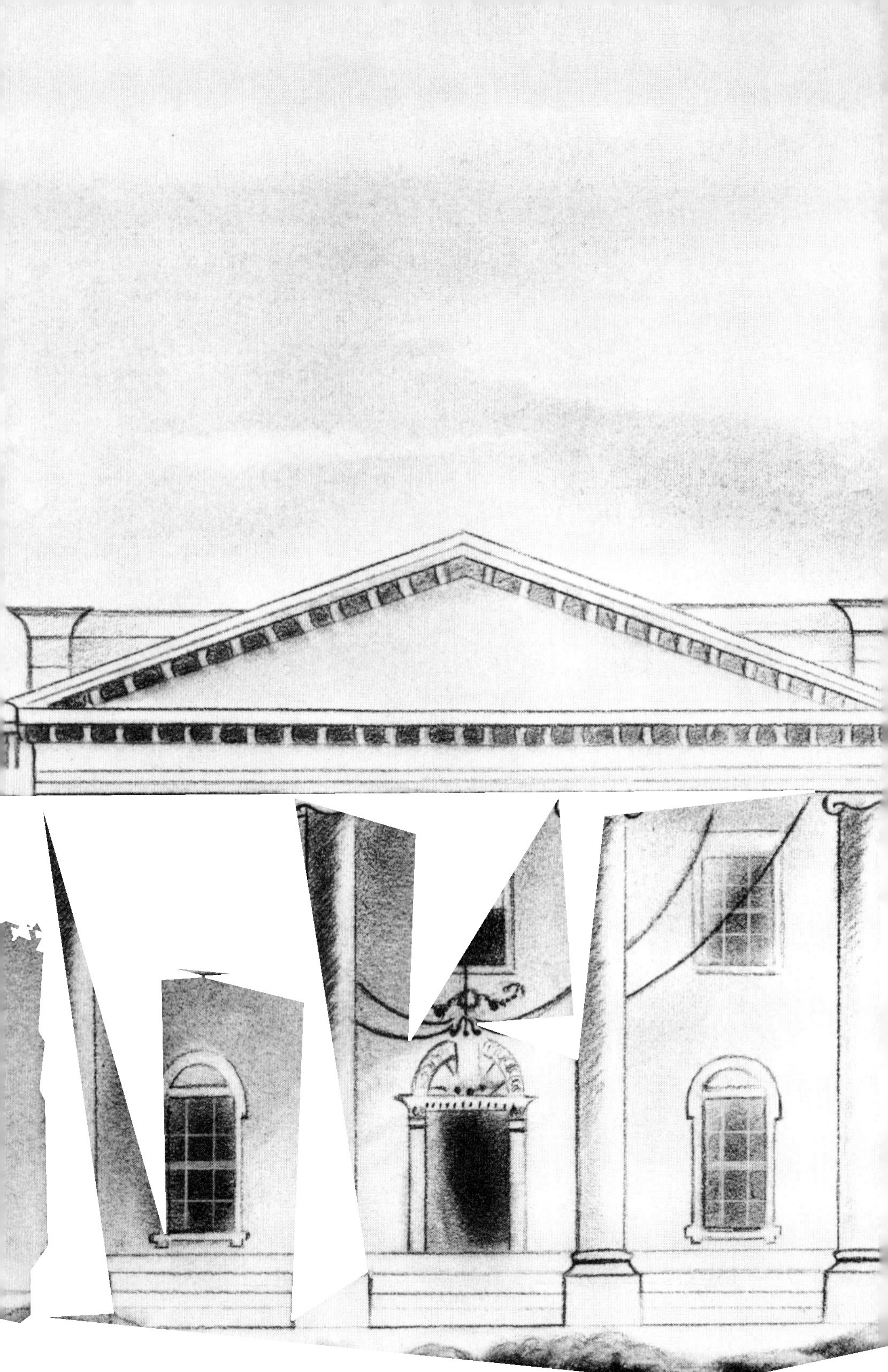

INTO THE THIRD CENTURY

THE PRESIDENCY

By

RICHARD B. BERNSTEIN

and

JEROME AGEL

WALKER AND COMPANY
NEW YORK

ST. PHILIP'S COLLEGE LIBRARY

Copyright © 1989 by Jerome Agel and Richard B. Bernstein

All rights reserved. No part of this book may be reproduced or transmitted in any form or by any means, electronic or mechanical, including photocopying, recording, or by any information storage and retrieval system, without permission in writing from the Publisher.

First published in the United States of America in 1989 by the Walker Publishing Company, Inc.

Published simultaneously in Canada by Thomas Allen & Son Canada, Limited, Markham, Ontario.

Library of Congress Cataloging-in-Publication Data

Bernstein, Richard B., 1956–
  Into the third century. The presidency / by Richard B. Bernstein and Jerome Agel.
    p. cm.
  Includes index.
  Summary: A history of the Presidency—how the Presidents have influenced history and how history has shaped the Presidency.
  ISBN 0-8027-6829-6. ISBN 0-8027-6831-8 (lib. bdg.)
  1. Presidents—United States—History—Juvenile literature. [1. Presidents—History.] I. Agel, Jerome. II. Title.
JK517.B47 1989
353.03'1'09—dc19   88-21026
                                                                           CIP
                                                                            AC

Printed in the United States of America

10 9 8 7 6 5 4 3 2 1

Into the Third Century

For my mother, my first teacher, with love.

R. B. B.

The Presidency

For Kathleen Spencer and Nathan Spencer . . . future leaders of the rising generation.

R. B. B.

CONTENTS

Introduction   ix

ONE | In the Shadow of Two Georges:
The Birth of the Presidency   1

TWO | Party Politics and Impartial Presidents:
From George Washington to John Quincy Adams   10

THREE | From Jackson to Buchanan   31

FOUR | Abraham Lincoln   42

FIVE | From Ford's Theatre to Exposition Hall   52

SIX | The Progressive Presidents:
Theodore Roosevelt, Taft, Wilson   64

SEVEN | The Republican Reign   75

EIGHT | Franklin D. Roosevelt   83

NINE | "Give 'em Hell, Harry" and "I Like Ike"   96

TEN | "The Challenging, Revolutionary Sixties":
Kennedy, Lyndon Johnson, Nixon   104

ELEVEN | Putting the Presidency Back Together:
Ford, Carter, Reagan   118

Into the Third Century   129

For Further Reading   133
Index   135

INTRODUCTION

The people of the United States govern themselves under a Constitution now two centuries old. It was written in the days of horse-drawn carriages and sailing ships, of powdered wigs and knee-breeches. Its authors, a few dozen men from twelve struggling states along the Atlantic Ocean, had never heard of personal computers or space satellites or nuclear reactors, of airplanes or railroads or automobiles.

The Constitution does not govern this country. "We the People of the United States" do that. We choose the people who will make our laws, enforce them, and settle disputes arising under them. Our Constitution establishes three branches of government: the legislative, the executive, and the judiciary. Each of these three branches has the power to check or restrain the other two branches. The three branches have often worked together and, just as often, they have worked against one another. They are held in a delicate balance by the commands of the Constitution. This system of government has turned out to be strong enough to deal with national problems, flexible enough to adapt to changing times and conditions, and limited enough to avoid damaging our rights.

This is one of three books about the central institutions of our system of government: Congress, the Presidency, and the Supreme Court. Reading all three volumes will introduce you to two centuries of American history, as well as to the history of each institution. You will also learn about the leading figures in each institution's history—the people who have helped to make our system of government work. Some important events appear in only one or two of the three books. This is because our system of government divides power among the three branches of our government. Therefore, some major problems in our history have been the business of only one branch or of two of the three.

CHAPTER ONE

IN THE SHADOW OF TWO GEORGES: THE BIRTH OF THE PRESIDENCY

On January 20, 1989, the forty-first President of the United States will swear the oath of office set forth in the Constitution—the same oath that George Washington took when he became the first President two hundred years ago.

We take the Presidency for granted. One political scientist wrote in the 1950s that most children know only two persons in government—the police officer on the corner and the President of the United States. Even when we grow up, we think of the President as the living symbol of our government, the central figure in our public life.

We think of the President as the most powerful person in the United States, and even in the world. We put our faith in the President and are slow to withdraw that faith even when the President is not up to the job. Some scholars even suggest that we expect more of the Presidency than any person or institution can possibly deliver.

It was not always this way. In fact, two hundred years ago, the American people debated whether we needed a President at all. To understand the Presidency, we have to go back to the beginnings of the office to see what ideas, fears, hopes, and doubts shaped it.

The Presidency was invented in the Assembly Room of the Pennsylvania State House—the building we now call Independence Hall—in Philadelphia in the spring and summer of 1787. Its inventors were a few dozen men from twelve of the thirteen original states, the delegates to the Federal Convention. (Rhode Island did not send delegates to the Convention.) These men thought long and hard about the troubles facing the new nation. Their job was to frame a document creating a new form of government for the United States of America. As they argued and scribbled and pondered, the delegates worried most about something they called *executive power*. An *executive* is a person in an organization, such as a government, who has the authority to make sure that things get done. Every form of government that the delegates to the Convention knew of had one person or a group of persons who exercised this executive power. What kind of executive was right for the United States?

The delegates knew their history. Several of them had spent another difficult spring and summer in that same room eleven years earlier, in 1776. They had been among the delegates to the Second Continental Congress, the group that had declared America's independence from Great Britain—a key step in the American Revolution. Many of the reasons for the American Revolution had to do with executive power and with abuses of that power. The delegates remembered that when their states were British colonies, the royal governors (chief executives appointed by the King far away in London) for no good reason had rejected, or *vetoed*, laws passed by the colonial legislatures. They also remembered that, when Parliament declared that it had the right to tax the colonists even though they were not represented in Parliament, King George III and his advisers had not supported the colonists.

George III had ignored every one of their appeals to him to defend their rights. When Thomas Jefferson drafted the Declaration of Independence, he made George III the villain—and the Continental Congress agreed with him. The shadow of George III hung over the Federal Convention.

The delegates also knew about the new states' experiments in government. Generally the new state constitutions adopted between 1776 and 1780 had cut back on executive power. One state, Pennsylvania, had even done away with an independent, one-person executive; its constitution set up a Supreme Executive Council under the thumb of the state's legislature. Most of the other states had a single executive, called a governor, but the governors were usually chosen by the legislatures and could be fired by the legislatures if they became too independent. As did the Second Continental Congress, the states' constitution-makers thought of George III as the villain.

Some Americans disagreed with this fear of executive power. John Adams of Massachusetts, a great lawyer and student of government, argued that a single executive was a necessary part of a government—*if* the government had built into it a system of separation of powers and checks and balances to make sure that the executive did not become a tyrant. When Adams wrote the first draft of the Massachusetts constitution of 1780, he put these ideas into practice. The state's governor would be elected by the people. He would have the power to veto laws passed by the legislature. He would command the armed forces of the state. He would have the power to appoint other state government officials, such as department heads and judges. A few other states, such as New York, adopted similar constitutions. The delegates to the Federal Convention knew about Adams's ideas and made use of them. (Adams himself was three thousand miles away, serving in London as the first American Minister to Great Britain.)

Adams's ideas had not shaped the new nation's first charter of government, the Articles of Confederation. Written in 1777 and adopted by the thirteenth and last state, Maryland, in 1781, the Articles of Confederation created only one institution of government, the Confederation Congress. This body had a president, but he was nothing like the President of the United States we know today, for he had almost no power.

The Articles of Confederation were too weak to work as a system of government. After years of frustration, the Confederation Congress and the state legislatures agreed that something had to be done. George Washington of Virginia, the retired Commander-in-Chief of the Continental Army and the most revered man in the nation, put it best in a private letter: "We are fast verging to anarchy and confusion!" And so the Confederation Congress authorized a convention to think about how to revise the Articles, and the legislatures of twelve states chose delegates to go to Philadelphia in the late spring of 1787.

One of the first things that the delegates decided was that revising the Articles would not be enough. They would have to start from the beginning; a whole new charter of government was needed. This new form of government should be responsible to the People of the United States. It should have the power to deal with national problems and to protect national interests. It should have all three elements of a fully organized system of government: a legislature, to make laws; an executive, to enforce the laws; and a judiciary, or court system, to settle disputes under the laws and interpret the laws.

The delegates decided these general issues quickly and with little argument. They spent most of their time and energy figuring out how each part of the system should work. They worried most of all about the executive. Their blueprint, the Virginia Plan drafted by James Madison, was silent on how the executive might be chosen or how many persons should make up the executive. When James Wilson of Pennsylvania suggested that there should be one chief executive, some delegates charged that Wilson was planting a seed that could grow into a monarchy. Other delegates disagreed, pointing out that the state governors had not become kings or tyrants. They reminded their colleagues that the Confederation could not pull itself together and speak with one voice for American interests. Surely the answer to this problem would be a one-man chief executive. Finally, the delegates voted in favor of a one-man chief executive, and they never looked back.

During the debate on the executive, the Convention's president, George Washington, looked on silently. Washington was one of seven Virginia delegates to the Convention, but Americans everywhere thought that he was their greatest man. He was honorable, honest, and able. He had led the Continental Army with dignity and resolve through the darkest days of the Revolution to victory and independence. He had rejected many attempts to make him king of America. At the war's end in December 1783, he had retired from public life to Mount Vernon, his beloved plantation on the Potomac River. He had gone to Philadelphia and put at risk his "harvest of glory" only because he believed that the problems facing the new nation were so great that they might destroy the success of the Revolution. He owed a duty to his country. His fellow delegates unanimously had elected him the Convention's president, and he justified their faith in him.

Washington must have known that the other delegates were looking at him while they discussed the chief executive—which they decided to call the President of the United States. He must have known that he almost certainly would be the first man to fill that office if the charter the delegates were drafting won the support of the people. And he must have known that, because the delegates trusted him, they were willing to take a gamble or two as they shaped the Presidency.

By September 17, 1787, the Constitution was finished, and thirty-nine of the forty-two delegates present signed it, led by George Washington. As Washington pored over the Constitution, he may well have read Article II with special care. Article II created the Presidency.

The President would be chosen for a term of four years by specially selected officials called *presidential electors*. The states would pick the electors (some states used their legislatures; others, such as Connecticut, relied on the people). The electors would vote for two men, at least one of whom could not be from their home state. A joint session of the House and the Senate would meet to count these *electoral votes*. The candidate with the most votes would become President, and the candidate with the second-highest number of votes would become Vice President. The Vice President would preside over the Senate and would take over for the President if the President should die, resign, or be removed from office.

The President's powers were not clearly defined. He would be pitted against the other two branches of government. He did have the power to appoint officers of government and federal judges—but the Senate had to approve his appointments. He could veto bills passed by Congress—but Congress could overturn his veto by a two-thirds vote of both the House of Representatives and the Senate. If he committed "treason, bribery, or other High Crimes and misdemeanors," the House could vote to *impeach* him (file formal charges against him); the Senate would try him on those charges and remove him from office by a two-thirds vote if they found him guilty. Still, the office of President of the United States had the potential to be what the holder of the office made of it. This potential was the result of the shadow of George Washington.

The delegates had managed to find a middle road between the two Georges: They were willing, by and large, to trust the

President, but they made sure that there were ways to limit his power and stop him in his tracks if he abused that power.

After the Federal Convention adjourned, a special messenger carried the Constitution by stagecoach to New York City, where the Confederation Congress was meeting. The Convention had adopted a special procedure for adopting the proposed new charter of government: Each state would hold elections for a special convention. These conventions would then vote whether to *ratify*, or adopt, the Constitution. If nine states' conventions ratified it, it would replace the Articles of Confederation.

After nearly a year of politicking and controversy, eleven states' conventions had adopted the Constitution. (The last two, North Carolina and Rhode Island, voted to ratify it in 1789 and 1790, respectively, after the charter had gone into effect.) During the ratification controversy, the Constitution's opponents, the Anti-Federalists, had charged that the President might become a tyrant like George III. The Constitution's supporters, the Federalists, answered that George Washington supported the Constitution and hinted that he would be the first President. They also argued that Congress and the judiciary would keep the President in line. The President, they said, was a necessary part of the active and vigorous national government the United States needed to stay free and independent.

By April 6, 1789, the Constitution was beginning its work as the new charter of government of the United States. The people had elected members of the House of Representatives. The state legislatures had chosen Senators and presidential electors. Now, in their first joint session, the House and Senate waited as the electoral votes were counted. To nobody's surprise, George Washington was the unanimous first choice for President, with all sixty-nine electoral votes. John Adams had only thirty-four of sixty-nine votes, but as the clear second-place candidate, he was the first Vice President.

Congress sent messengers to Virginia and Massachusetts, respectively, to inform Washington and Adams of their election.

Washington was not pleased by the news. He knew that his election had been certain—even though in this first Presidential "contest" there were no official candidates and no active campaigns for office. He wrote, "My feelings upon assuming this office are not unlike those of a culprit going to the place of execution." He knew that he was about to assume a crushing burden. Everything he did or did not do—every statement, every act, every failure to act—would set a precedent for everyone who filled the office of President after him. He was about to lead his country into unexplored territory.

Washington was one of the richest men in the United States, but he had so little cash on hand that he had to borrow money to finance his trip to the inauguration in New York City, the nation's first capital. He was greeted by cheering crowds every step of his journey north. His arrival in New York City on April 23, 1789, was marked by a thunderous demonstration of the love, trust, and support of the American people. (John Adams had arrived more quietly a few days before and on April 21 had been sworn in as the Vice President.) A week of ceremonies and preparations led up to the first Presidential inauguration, on April 30, 1789.

Chancellor Robert R. Livingston of New York, one of that state's highest judges, swore in the new President. (There were no federal judges yet because Congress had not yet written the law setting up the federal courts.) The ceremony took place on the balcony of Federal Hall, the new capitol of the United States. A huge crowd of people watched, expectant and proud, at the corner of Wall Street and Broad Street. Washington took pains to give the right impression in his first public appearance as President. He refused to wear his army uniform, choosing instead a suit of brown American-made broadcloth to show his support for American industry. At the last moment, the officials on the balcony of Federal Hall realized that there was no Bible on hand for the ceremony. A messenger hurried around the corner to a Masonic lodge to borrow its Bible. After the grave and composed Washington took the oath, every church bell in New York City pealed forth. Chancellor Livingston shouted: "God save George Washington, President of the United States!" The people cheered and threw their hats and bouquets of flowers into the air.

Inside Federal Hall, Washington delivered his Inaugural Address to a joint session of the House and Senate. But, to the surprise of the new First Congress, the man who had braved cannon fire and battle in a long and distinguished military career read his speech in a trembling voice and with shaking hands. One Pennsylvania Senator, William Maclay, wrote in his diary that he was crushed that his hero "was not first in everything."

The glorious display of fireworks that evening, the finest ever seen in America, dispelled the Senators' and Representatives' surprise at Washington's nervousness. Everyone felt pride that the great American experiment of self-government was under way.

CHAPTER TWO

PARTY POLITICS AND IMPARTIAL PRESIDENTS: FROM GEORGE WASHINGTON TO JOHN QUINCY ADAMS

Professor Ralph Ketcham, a leading expert on the first four decades of the Presidency, has shown that our first six Presidents believed that a President should be President of all the people. He should not be associated with any special group, political party, or interest. He should try to govern the country in the national interest and for the general good.

George Washington took great care to act as an impartial, nonpartisan President. He was careful to defer to Congress. He did not propose legislation—that was the job of Congress. Once Congress passed laws creating the departments of government (State, Treasury, and War), the President's aides worked with Congress to make policy. Washington merely kept an eye on the process. His job was to carry out the will of Congress, to enforce the laws, to oversee the running of the government, to act as the symbol of the nation, and to uphold the values of the Constitution. Washington took great care to carry out these tasks with care and good judgment.

The President knew that he was not a brilliant man, but he knew who the brilliant men were, and he brought them into the government. He worked closely with Representative

James Madison of Virginia. He relied on his longtime friend and wartime aide Secretary of the Treasury Alexander Hamilton of New York, Secretary of War Henry Knox of Massachusetts, and two more of his fellow Virginians—Thomas Jefferson, the Secretary of State, and young, able, but erratic Attorney General Edmund Randolph. These four men made up the President's *Cabinet*—a term borrowed from British politics of the period to mean the President's leading advisers. Washington also named his old friend John Jay of New York to be the first Chief Justice of the United States and took great pains in naming the other federal judges as well.

In choosing federal officials, from the highest post to the lowest, the President used three rules of thumb: He wanted the best-qualified candidates; he wanted supporters of the Constitution in the ratification controversy; and he wanted geographical balance so that no one could say that any state or region dominated the new government.

Washington pondered issues of policy, requested reports and opinions from his principal advisers, and gathered advice from as many sources as possible before making up his mind. Jefferson declared, long after Washington's death in 1799, that the President's judgment "was slow in operation, but none was ever sounder."

All these men, not just President Washington, were operating "in a wilderness without a path to guide us," as James Madison complained. There were times when they simply did not know what to do. At one point in his first months as Chief Executive, Washington appeared in person before the Senate to lay a treaty before them and seek their advice and consent. The embarrassed Senators sat silently for a while, then asked the President if they could consider the matter and send him their answer. Washington stalked from the chamber, furious and humiliated, and told his secretary, Tobias Lear, that he would never go back there again. And he never did.

Similarly, in 1793, Washington and Jefferson tried to get advice from the Justices of the Supreme Court about whether certain measures to protect American neutrality during a brewing European war would be constitutional, but Chief Justice Jay and his colleagues respectfully refused. They explained that the Constitution permitted the federal courts only to give opinions on actual disputes, not to give advice. In this way, feeling things out step by step and making an occasional mistake, the Washington Administration reshaped American politics to fit within the framework of the Constitution.

One thing that nobody expected—not Washington nor any of his advisers nor anyone else in American politics—was the development of institutions that we now take for granted as an essential part of our system of government: political parties. Most politicians in this period believed that they should discuss issues of policy together to achieve what was best for the nation as a whole. They believed that political parties were selfish groups of people who wanted to advance themselves and not the common good. But different groups had different ideas of what the common good was, and as a result they created organizations that were the nation's first political parties.

Two issues shaped the first political parties under the Constitution. The first was the dispute over the economic policies advocated by Treasury Secretary Hamilton. Hamilton was trying to solve the problem of the huge federal and state debts left over from the Revolution. His complex and daring proposals were designed to give the new nation a stable currency, to systematize the various debts crushing the economy, and to give a badly needed boost to American commercial and manufacturing interests. But his critics, led by Madison and Jefferson, charged that Hamilton was favoring the wealthy Eastern interests at the expense of the rest of the nation. They said that he was bending the Constitution out of shape in order to make the national government more powerful. In addition, they claimed, manufacturing and commerce were fine for Europe, but farming was the only fit way of life for Americans who wanted to preserve their freedoms.

The other catalyst of parties was foreign policy—specifically, American reactions to the French Revolution that had begun in 1789 and toppled King Louis XVI. The crowned heads of Europe soon led their nations into war against the revolutionary French government. Many Americans believed that the overthrow of the French monarchy and nobility was only the first outbreak of a worldwide revolutionary movement that would result in government by the people in every nation on earth. Jefferson, Madison, and their allies welcomed this possibility. They argued that the United States should support the French, in part because of the 1778 treaty between the United States and France that had resulted in decisive French military aid to the American revolution. Hamilton, John Adams, John Jay, and those who agreed with them feared that revolutionary zeal might overthrow good governments as well as bad. They believed that Great Britain, which had been our foe during the Revolution, was leading the forces of civilization against disorder. And President Washington worried that the United States was still too weak to risk getting pulled into what was becoming a world war. For this reason, the President in 1793 proclaimed that the United States would be neutral as to the war raging in Europe.

The battle lines were drawn. If you opposed the French Revolution or favored neutrality, supported Hamilton, and favored a strong national government, you were a Federalist. (These Federalists were different from the Federalists of 1787–1788, who had supported the Constitution during the ratification controversy.) If you supported the French Revolution, opposed Hamilton, and favored limiting the powers of the national government, you were a Republican.

Parties were becoming central to American politics, and

President Washington was disheartened by this development. In the spring of 1792, as the government was settling into its quarters in Philadelphia and the nation's second Presidential election approached, he determined to retire. Divided on most other issues, Jefferson and Hamilton agreed that it was vital for the President to continue in office. Washington reluctantly gave in to their pleas. The Electoral College once again elected him unanimously, but he took no joy in winning another four years of holding the nation together.

On the home front, Washington and Hamilton were confronted with a direct challenge to the power of the United States. Farmers in western Pennsylvania refused to pay the federal tax on whiskey adopted as part of Hamilton's financial policies. They depended on distilling whiskey from their surplus grain to make ends meet and resented a tax that would cut back on their profits. Now they were taking up their guns to resist federal agents who had been sent into Pennsylvania to collect the whiskey tax. Hamilton was outraged by the farmers' defiance of federal authority. He persuaded the President that drastic measures were called for. A 13,000-man army composed of militia from four states was called together on Presidential authority, and President Washington donned his uniform and in his constitutional role of Commander-in-Chief took the field to command this army to crush the "Whiskey Rebellion." The show of force worked, and the "rebels" melted away. But Republicans were alarmed, fearing that this army would be used to suppress them as well. Although the army quickly disbanded after the rebellion's end, Republicans remembered and resented the President's resort to force.

By 1796, Washington was in his mid-sixties and so tired and disgusted with politics that he was adamant about stepping down from the Presidency. Both Jefferson and Hamilton had retired during his second term, and the President felt abandoned. Washington also began to take the Republican party's pro-French and anti-Administration stand personally. He believed that the Republicans were undercutting his authority, questioning his honesty and patriotism, and endangering the Constitution. "The spirit of party" was fostering geographic schisms and foreign intrigues. He had had enough.

Washington asked Hamilton to prepare a farewell address and discussed what it should say with the brilliant New Yorker. The President then took Hamilton's draft and completely reworked it so that it expressed his ideas in his own words. The Farewell Address first appeared in two pages in a four-page Philadelphia newspaper, David Claypoole's *American*

George Washington (1789–1797) was the first of only two Presidents to take the field as Commander-in-Chief. In 1794, he reviewed militiamen on their way to force angry farmers in western Pennsylvania to pay federal taxes on home-distilled spirits. The suppression of the Whiskey Rebellion vindicated the authority of the national government.

Daily Advertiser, on September 19, 1796. In it, he expressed his hope that the nation would continue on a virtuous path, leading the rest of the world to liberty. It was Washington's most important statement of his views as a political thinker and has had lasting influence. Today we value Washington's advice about foreign policy, good government, and national union, but in 1796 the Republicans resented the President's charges that they were threatening the stability of the nation. Washington did not care what they thought. He was going home, relieved to be rid of the cares and frustrations of office.

Washington did something else important by stepping down from the Presidency. His decision that two terms were enough established a rule for his successors that lasted for nearly 150 years: the "two-term tradition."

With Washington's retirement, the nation faced its first Presidential election in which political parties chose candidates to compete for the job. Informal meetings of leading Federalists and Republicans chose each party's candidates. The Federalists rallied behind Vice President John Adams; the Republicans backed former Secretary of State Thomas Jefferson. The Electoral College chose Adams to be the second President. His defeated opponent, Jefferson, was the runner-up—and thus became the new Vice President.

Adams and Jefferson had been close friends for two decades, but now they were political rivals, their friendship in ruins. Similarly, Alexander Hamilton and James Madison had been friends and allies in the task of framing and adopting the Constitution, but they parted ways under the pressure of party strife. The years from 1797 to 1801 were difficult for all these men, and for the nation.

On March 4, 1797, as John Adams was taking the Presidential oath of office, he noticed Washington's gaze fixed upon him. The outgoing President seemed to be saying, "Aye, I am fairly out and you are fairly in. We will see which of us is happier." The pessimistic Adams worried about the burdens he would face. He had already spent eight years as understudy to the most revered man in the United States—a daunting task for even the strongest personality. Adams was usually a stubborn, independent man, not afraid to speak his mind no matter what the result. He also believed that he was smarter than Washington. But the new President was nervous about doing anything that might be taken as criticism of Washington. Thus, he kept on Washington's advisers as his own. This turned out to be a major mistake, for in his second term Washington had picked his Cabinet based on the advice of Alexander Hamilton. The Federalist Party was split between Hamilton men and Adams men. The Cabinet was filled with friends and supporters of the former Treasury Secretary, and Hamilton still "pulled the strings." Meanwhile, President Adams, not realizing who was *really* running his government, spent months at a time at his home in Massachusetts.

The Adams Administration's most serious problems had to do with foreign policy. War was raging across the Atlantic between the French Revolutionary government and the European powers led by Great Britain. The United States was neutral in this war, following President Washington's 1793 proclamation, but French ships had begun to harass and even to capture American ships sailing to and from British ports.

President Adams decided to send a delegation to France to try to stop French plunder of American shipping. He appointed two Federalists, Charles C. Pinckney of South Carolina and John Marshall of Virginia, and one Republican, Elbridge Gerry of Massachusetts. Pinckney, Marshall, and Gerry cooled their heels in frustration as French Foreign Minister Talleyrand kept them waiting. Finally, the three Americans were approached by three middle-level French officials, who hinted that the Americans would have to bribe them to ensure progress in the American-French negotiations. Pinckney, Marshall, and Gerry were outraged. Pinckney declared: "No, no, not a sixpence!" The three Americans sent John Marshall home with their report on the bribe offer by the French agents, code named X, Y, and Z in the report.

Marshall was given a hero's welcome. The President released Marshall's report to Congress, and the "XYZ Affair" infuriated the American people. The Republicans, who had supported the French Revolutionary cause, were disgusted with the French blunder. The Federalists, who believed that Great Britain and the other allies were fighting for the cause of civilization against the French menace, were delighted. They adopted as their slogan the phrase "Millions for defense; not one cent for tribute!"

Calls for war went up throughout the nation, but Adams adopted a more moderate course. He got authorization from Congress to direct the American Navy to take action against French ships that menaced American shipping. This was our first *undeclared* war—that is, the first military conflict that Congress did not begin by declaring war as provided by the Constitution.

The Federalists in Congress rammed through two bills, quickly signed into law by President Adams, that were intended to protect American security at home. The Alien Act made it more difficult for people from foreign countries to become American citizens and gave the federal government the power to *deport*, or throw out, foreign subjects residing in the United States. The Sedition Act made it a crime to criticize the President or other officers of the government. The Federalists used the Sedition Act to prosecute and jail critics of President Adams and the war.

The Republicans struck back at the Alien and Sedition Acts. The legislatures of Virginia and Kentucky passed resolutions claiming that these laws were unconstitutional. The Kentucky Resolutions, secretly written by Vice President Jefferson, declared as well that these acts were null and void within the state of Kentucky. The Virginia Resolutions, secretly the work of former Representative Madison, declared that Virginia would resist federal attempts to enforce these laws until the other states helped to settle the issue whether they were constitutional. No other state supported the Virginia and Kentucky legislatures, but the Republicans skillfully linked the Federalist Party, and President Adams, with the hated Alien and Sedition Acts.

Adams also called for the assembling of an army in case the French should actually invade the United States. He called George Washington out of retirement to lead this army. But the former President set a condition for his service that made the President cringe—Washington demanded that Hamilton be named his second-in-command. Adams gave in, but this army never saw action.

In late 1799 and early 1800, the President discovered that Hamilton secretly had been running his Cabinet and thus the government. In a towering rage, Adams confronted his Cabinet and forced all of them to resign. He surrounded himself with advisers who were loyal to him. He also sent Chief Justice Oliver Ellsworth, William Vans Murray, and William R. Davie to France to negotiate an end to the undeclared naval war. Adams thus saved the nation from a full-scale war, the goal of the Hamiltonian Federalists. But the President had destroyed his political career, for the vindictive "High" Federalists were now sworn to cost him the Presidency in the election of 1800.

The 1800 Presidential election once again pitted John Adams against his Vice President, Thomas Jefferson. But the harshest attacks against the President came from Alexander Hamilton, who recklessly wrote and published a furious pamphlet against Adams. This pamphlet played into the hands of Jefferson's supporters.

By now, both political parties had learned to designate Presidential and Vice Presidential candidates. Until 1824, political parties picked their candidates by gatherings of party leaders (*caucuses*) in Congress. Adams's "running-mate" was

Major General Charles C. Pinckney of South Carolina; Jefferson's was Senator Aaron Burr of New York. Hamilton and his allies worked to ensure that Adams would not win a second term. They hoped to elect Pinckney, whom they could influence. But their strategy backfired. Both Adams and Pinckney were soundly beaten by the Republican ticket.

But the Republican victory was flawed. Somehow, nobody had made certain that the Republican electors would give Jefferson more votes than Burr. Thus, each man received seventy-three electoral votes—a tie for the Presidency. Under the Constitution, the House of Representatives, with each state voting as a unit, had the task of picking the new President if there were a tie in the electoral votes or if no one candidate received a clear majority. Ballot after ballot failed to break the deadlock.

The Federalist Representatives held themselves aloof from the voting, trying to figure out which of the two men to support. Watching from the sidelines, Hamilton realized that he had helped to cause this mess by undercutting Adams and thought long and hard about the advice that he should give his Federalist colleagues. He decided to tell them to vote for Jefferson. Jefferson was an honest man, even though the Federalists disliked his politics; by contrast, Hamilton distrusted Burr's ideas and doubted his honor. The Federalist Representatives moved into line, and Jefferson was finally elected, ten states to four, with two not voting.

During all this, President Adams sulked, sad and bitter, in the Executive Mansion in Washington, D.C. He had averted a disastrous war with France, only to be betrayed—as he saw it—by his own party. He feared for the future of the country. But there were still several weeks left before Adams and the old Congress had to leave office. They now worked together to create dozens of federal judgeships and to appoint deserving Federalists to those posts. At least the Federalists would keep control of one branch of the government. President Adams stayed up till long after midnight on his last day in office, signing and sealing the commissions of the last batch of judicial appointees. (Republicans angrily nicknamed these men the "midnight judges.") On the morning of March 4, 1801, Inauguration Day, President Adams left Washington, D.C., choosing not to attend Jefferson's swearing-in. Adams, the first President to live in the new capital city, was glad to know that he would never have to return.

Thomas Jefferson awakened on Inauguration Day in his boarding house, dressed, and walked along Pennsylvania Avenue—a mud-lined dirt track in those days—to the unfinished Capitol building. There, his distant cousin and political enemy, Chief Justice John Marshall, administered the Presidential oath of office. Jefferson delivered an eloquent Inaugural Address but, because he was a poor orator who hated and feared public speaking, he could not be heard beyond the first few rows of the audience. Once the ceremony was over, Jefferson shook hands with friends and supporters and walked back to his rooming house, where he had to wait to be seated for lunch. Government was simple and primitive in the first years of the nineteenth century. Jefferson was determined to make this simplicity the theme of his Administration.

Jefferson was proud of his victory over Adams and the Federalists. He called it a revolution, and in a way it was. It was the first time under the Constitution that power had shifted from one political party to another. But the credit for this achievement rests, in the end, with the Federalists. Although they had controlled the machinery of government, they did not try to prevent the lawful transfer of power to the Republicans.

Jefferson's "Revolution of 1800" did not change the direction of public policy, as he had hoped. Hamilton's economic system, now more than a decade old, could not be abolished or replaced. Jefferson mourned that the national debt could be paid off in ten years, "but we can never get rid of his system." The President also found that he could not stick to his view that the Constitution gave the federal government only specific, limited powers. Here, too, Hamilton's ideas prevailed.

The most famous instance when President Jefferson was obliged to go beyond the words of the Constitution was the Louisiana Purchase. In 1802, Spain transferred to France ownership of the land on both sides of the lower Mississippi River and the city of New Orleans. For nearly twenty years, Americans had tried to buy New Orleans for the new nation to ensure access to the river and the Gulf of Mexico for western settlers who depended on the Mississippi to ship their goods and crops. But Spain had resisted. Now Jefferson thought that France might be willing to deal. He sent two diplomats, James Monroe of Virginia and Robert R. Livingston of New York, to Paris to negotiate with Emperor Napoleon I and the durable Count Talleyrand. It turned out that Napoleon had no desire for vast American possessions. He needed money to finance his European wars. He thus offered to sell New Orleans *and* the whole Louisiana Territory to the United States for $15 million—about two-and-one-half cents per acre. (It was an area larger than the combined areas of France, Germany, Italy, Spain, and Portugal.) Monroe and Livingston were delighted but uncertain. They sent word of Napoleon's proposal back to Jefferson, who also was unsure. Nothing in the Constitution specifically authorized the federal government to enter into a treaty to purchase land. Jefferson even drafted a proposed constitutional amendment to authorize the deal. But in the end Jefferson and his Secretary of State, James Madison, decided that the deal was constitutional because the Constitution's words did not *forbid* treaties of this kind.

The treaty, ratified by the Senate in 1803, more than doubled the size of the United States. (Because of the huge outlay for the Louisiana Purchase, the President felt that the

United States did not have the money to buy Cuba, also for sale.) To find out what benefits the Louisiana Territory held for the United States, the President, under a $2,500 grant authorized by Congress, sent out his private secretary, Captain Meriwether Lewis, and Lieutenant William Clark to explore the region, where no white man had gone before, and to discover a water passage to the Pacific—the age-long search for the Northwest Passage. The Lewis and Clark Expedition discovered 24 Indian tribes, 178 plants, and 122 animals previously unknown to the civilized world, established the U.S. claim to the Oregon territory, and sailed the Snake and Columbia rivers to the Pacific Ocean—a 4,000-mile round trip with the loss of only one man (due to a ruptured appendix). Jefferson's decision to send out this scientific expedition further expanded the powers of the federal government and the Presidency, and expanded the nation's destiny westward.

In dealing with the Barbary Pirates, the President also found himself forced to exercise powers not specifically prohibited by the Constitution. These pirates, based in North Africa, sailed the Mediterranean, seizing ships and hostages from nations that refused to pay them *tribute*, or protection money. They held these ships and hostages for ransom. Other nations had bought off the Barbary Pirates, but for nearly thirty years the United States had refused to do so—both out of principle and for the practical reason that the new nation could not afford tribute or ransom. Finally, President Jefferson sent a naval expedition, commanded by Lieutenant Stephen Decatur, who led a detachment of U.S. Marines across the desert and surprised the pirates at their headquarters in Tripoli. The Americans broke the power of the Barbary Pirates.

The Presidential election of 1804, in which Thomas Jefferson was triumphantly re-elected for a second term, was the first governed by the new Twelfth Amendment to the Constitution. This amendment, ratified just before the election, was designed to prevent a replay of the Jefferson-Burr tie four years earlier. It required the members of the Electoral College to vote separately for President and Vice President.

Jefferson had a new Vice President for his second term, George Clinton of New York, who had been the state's governor for all but six years between 1777 and 1804. The Republicans had silently agreed to "dump" Vice President Burr. Nobody in the party or in Jefferson's Administration trusted Burr after the drawn-out election of 1800. He decided to switch parties in 1802 and ran against Clinton as the Federalist candidate for Governor of New York, but Hamilton engineered Burr's defeat.

The forty-seven-year-old Burr and the forty-nine-year-old Hamilton had much in common. Both were short and brilliant, both were polished speakers and able lawyers, and both were popular with the ladies. The two men grew to loathe each other. Hamilton's son Philip was killed in a duel with a Burr supporter in 1801, and the heartbroken Hamilton felt responsible for his son's death. In 1804, Hamilton recklessly denounced Burr as a politician and attacked his private character as well. Angered, Burr demanded an explanation, which Hamilton refused to give. Burr finally "demanded satisfaction"—a standard phrase of that time for a challenge to a duel—and Hamilton agreed to meet Burr on the "field of honor." On July 11, 1804, the two men faced each other, pistols in hand, across a dueling field on a narrow tree-bowered ledge of Weehawken Heights, New Jersey, on the banks of the Hudson River. Hamilton's shot went wild. Burr's shot mortally wounded Hamilton, who died in agony the next day.

Dueling was illegal in New York, and a New York grand jury indicted Burr for defying the law. A New Jersey grand jury indicted Burr for murder, though the dueling laws were not enforced in that state. The Vice President found refuge in

Philadelphia and then fled to the South, where he was welcomed as a hero in a region that considered dueling to be an honorable custom among gentlemen. But Federalists and Republicans joined forces in denouncing Burr, whose political career crumbled into ruins. (Eventually, the grand jury indictments faded away and were forgotten.) Hamilton was briefly honored as a martyr and then largely forgotten.

In his last days as Vice President, Burr helped to strangle one of President Jefferson's most important projects. The President was bitter about the Federalists' takeover of the federal courts. He and Secretary of State James Madison had refused to deliver judicial commissions to some of the "midnight judges" appointed by President Adams, but the scheme backfired. In a landmark 1803 case, *Marbury v. Madison,* Chief Justice John Marshall had asserted that the Supreme Court had the power to decide whether federal laws violated the Constitution. Jefferson and his allies in Congress decided to use the constitutional power of impeachment to clear Federalists out of the judiciary. They argued that impeachment was simply a process to determine whether someone holding a federal office should be replaced—not a way to punish a federal office-holder for violating the law or abusing his power. The Jeffersonians in Congress managed to oust old, senile, drunken Judge John Pickering of the federal district court in New Hampshire, but their effort to remove Supreme Court Justice Samuel Chase failed in the Senate. Vice President Burr presided over the Senate's trial of Justice Chase. He conducted it with strict fairness, and the Senators voted to acquit the Justice. Jefferson was furious but could do nothing.

Jefferson's second term was more difficult than his first. As another round of wars engulfed Europe, the President was determined to keep the United States neutral and at peace. He declared an *embargo,* or ban on trade, with all the warring European powers. He hoped that the loss of American trade would force the Europeans to bring the war to an end. But

French and British warships raided American ships trading with neutral nations, and American merchants suffered terribly.

Aaron Burr was still causing trouble for the President as well. Federal authorities arrested Burr in Alabama in the western territories. Jefferson believed that Burr had been plotting to lead an armed conquest of the Louisiana Territory, the western states, and Mexico in order to create a new empire with himself as emperor. Attorney General George Hay followed Jefferson's orders and prosecuted Burr for treason and conspiracy in the U.S. Circuit Court in Virginia. Chief Justice John Marshall presided over the trial. Marshall and Jefferson got into another tangle when Burr's lawyers issued a formal order, or *subpoena*, demanding that the President be called as a witness and that he produce government documents. Jefferson refused to testify, but he turned over most of the documents that Burr had requested and that Marshall had ordered produced. Historians are still unsure what Burr's real hopes or plans were, and it is likely that Burr had no idea himself. In any event, to Jefferson's alarm and fury, Burr was acquitted on the charge of treason. The former Vice President sailed for Europe, a crushed man; he lived thirty more years but never again had influence in American politics.

In 1808, Jefferson decided that he would not seek a third term. He was tired of public life, and he agreed with Washington that no President should serve more than two terms in office. Secretary of State James Madison became the Republican Presidential candidate and handily defeated Federalist Charles C. Pinckney.

The new President was short, quiet, and reserved, and in some ways a more realistic politician than Jefferson had been. He lifted Jefferson's embargo on trading with warring countries, delighting merchants along the Eastern coast. But the European war continued, and American shipping still suffered at the hands of British warships. When British officers seized, or *impressed,* American sailors to replace British sailors who had been killed in battle, died on the high seas, or jumped ship, Madison and the Republicans in Congress believed that going to war with Great Britain was the only way to preserve American independence. In 1812, the President sent a message to Congress asking for a declaration of war because of British interference with American shipping. Congress answered Madison's call before word arrived that the British had repealed the "orders in council" authorizing these attacks.

Some pro-war Americans enthusiastically called the new three-year war "the Second War for Independence," but most later historians simply call it the War of 1812. Radical members of the House of Representatives, such as Henry Clay of Kentucky and John C. Calhoun of South Carolina, demanded that the American army conquer Canada to add it to the Union and to deny the British a valuable base for military operations in the Western Hemisphere. But the American military expeditions to Canada ended in disaster for the United States. Other American military operations had mixed results. After a few brilliant victories, the American Navy was bottled up by a British blockade. British armies trounced American forces in most of their battles. The low point for the United States came in 1814 when a British force captured and burned Washington, D.C., in revenge for the Americans' burning of the Parliament building in Toronto. Madison was forced to flee for his life; he watched from the Virginia hills as the capital burned. His wife, Dolley Madison, remained at the Executive Mansion long enough to save several priceless objects from destruction, including Gilbert Stuart's official portrait of George Washington.

The War of 1812 ended as inconclusively as it had begun. American and British diplomats meeting in the city of Ghent, Belgium, agreed on a treaty that left things pretty much as they had been when the war started. Two weeks after the treaty was signed, but long before that news reached the

United States, a British army besieged New Orleans. The American commander, General Andrew Jackson, aided by the French pirate Jean Lafitte, directed the American defense. The tiny American force inflicted a shattering defeat on the British, and Jackson became a national hero. President Madison also basked in the glory of the Battle of New Orleans—though it had been a useless battle, a fitting end to a largely useless war.

Madison's greatest domestic problem during the War of 1812 was connected to the war. In the first days of "war fever," he easily won a second term in the Presidential election of 1812. But the New England states, the last stronghold of the disintegrating Federalist Party, soon became grim and discontented about the war. The New England Federalists hated the war because it was choking their trade and profits, and they felt a natural sympathy for Great Britain. The five New England states resisted the government's calls for soldiers and supplies. Some New England politicians even suggested that their states leave the Union, or *secede,* to form their own country or to return to the British Empire. They called a convention to meet at Hartford, Connecticut, but the Hartford Convention broke up in disarray when news of the Treaty of Ghent and the Battle of New Orleans arrived.

President Madison announced his retirement after two terms, reinforcing the "no third term" tradition of Washington and Jefferson. His Secretary of State, James Monroe of Virginia, won a landslide victory in 1816 over the last Federalist Presidential candidate, Rufus King of Massachusetts. Monroe was the fifth President, the fourth to come from Virginia. During his first term, the Federalist party finally dissolved. In 1820, Monroe ran unopposed for a second term. One Presidential elector (William Plumer of New Hampshire) cast his vote for Secretary of State John Quincy Adams, however, arguing that only George Washington deserved the honor of being elected to the Presidency unanimously.

Monroe's most famous achievement, known today as the Monroe Doctrine, was actually the work of Secretary of State John Quincy Adams. Monroe and Adams were responding to the breakup of the Spanish Empire in the Western Hemisphere. Spain's colonies, inspired by the American and French Revolutions, threw off the rule of their mother country and established themselves as republics. Spain was determined to reconquer its former colonies, but Great Britain opposed Spain's plans. The British suggested that they and the United States issue a joint guarantee of the independence of the new Latin American republics. But President Monroe and Secretary Adams resisted these British efforts to direct the affairs of Latin America. In December 1823, Monroe sent his sixth annual message to Congress. He warned all European powers not to interfere in the affairs of the Western Hemisphere. If any nation would guarantee the independence of the nations of the region, it would be the United States. This was the Monroe Doctrine.

By 1824, the "no third term" rule laid down by George Washington had become a tradition. James Monroe gladly retired to private life. His eight years in office had become known as the "Era of Good Feeling" because of his popularity. But Monroe's retirement made clear that the Republican Party was badly divided, and in the 1824 Presidential election it broke apart. Four candidates battled to become the sixth President: Secretary of State Adams, the candidate of the National Republicans; General Andrew Jackson, backed by the newly formed Democrats; William Crawford, the choice of Republicans in the House and Senate; and Henry Clay.

When the electoral votes were counted, no candidate had a majority. Jackson led with ninety-nine electoral votes; Adams had eighty-four; Crawford had forty-one; and Clay had thirty-seven. (Crawford actually was out of the running; he had suffered several crippling strokes.) The House of Representatives once again would have to choose the next

President. There is still controversy over what happened in the House, but we do know that Clay endorsed Adams. Thus, Adams was able to defeat Jackson in the House. He then named Clay his Secretary of State. Jackson's infuriated supporters charged that a "corrupt bargain" had taken place. They planned to punish Adams and Clay in the next election, in 1828.

John Quincy Adams was one of the most able men ever to become President. He had been one of the greatest Secretaries of State the United States has ever had. Adams was an imaginative man with wide-ranging interests and talents. If he had had a chance, he would have been one of our greatest Presidents. But, like his father, John Adams, he was stubborn, independent, and out of touch with the American people. When an Englishman named James Smithson died and left his fortune to the United States to be used "for the increase and diffusion of knowledge among men," Adams proposed the creation of what we now call the Smithsonian Institution—despite the demands of Senators and Representatives that the money be used to found an agricultural college or even be put straight into the U.S. Treasury. Years passed before Adams's views prevailed. History proved him right, but in this and many other controversies he could not win popular support for his views.

By 1828, the use of the Congressional caucus as a way to select Presidential and Vice Presidential candidates had ended. Instead, political parties held conventions at which party leaders and delegates from state party organizations picked the candidates.

The year 1828 marked the end of the American Presidency as a nonpartisan office that would identify and serve the common good. In the dawn of a new era of politics, President Adams lost his bid for a second term. Andrew Jackson ran as the common man's candidate and triumphed.

CHAPTER THREE

FROM JACKSON TO BUCHANAN

Andrew Jackson was a gaunt, ill-tempered man. His opponents thought that he was a barbarian or a savage. He had fought duels, and he had hanged men. In 1828, he was racked by illnesses that left him weighing only 127 pounds though he was six feet tall. But his iron will kept him going even when most physicians wondered that he was still alive. This force of will enabled him to dominate American politics for eight years.

Andrew Jackson went to his inauguration in 1829 wearing black, for he still mourned the death several months earlier of his beloved wife, Rachel. When Andrew and Rachel Jackson wed, both believed that Rachel had been divorced from her first husband. But Rachel's husband had not carried out the legal formalities. When he disclosed this fact, the heartbroken Rachel Jackson took to her bed and died. Jackson, anguished and bitter, blamed her death on his political enemies. He was in an unforgiving mood as he assumed the Presidency.

Inauguration Day, 1829, was a triumph for the common man that quickly got out of hand. Jackson had invited his supporters to the Executive Mansion, and they came in droves, stomping muddy footprints all over the carpeting and furniture, breaking windows, and passing out drunk in the East Room. Friends helped the President escape from the crush through an open window.

In an election as in a war, Jackson argued, "to the victors belong the spoils." In this case, the "spoils" were government jobs. Jackson named loyal supporters to those jobs regardless of the men's abilities. His opponents were outraged but helpless. Jackson thus solidified the *spoils system* that lasted for more than half a century, until passage of the Federal Service Act in 1883.

President Jackson also acted from constitutional principle. In his first term, the most important issue was an old standby in American politics: Did Congress have the power under the Constitution to establish a national bank? The means to create a bank was to issue a document called a *charter*. Congress had voted to renew the charter of the Second Bank of the United States, based in Philadelphia. But Jackson believed that the Bank was a bastion of wealth and privilege oppressing ordinary Americans. He also believed that, because the Constitution did not specifically authorize Congress to charter a bank, Congress did not have this power. For these reasons, which he set forth in a biting message to Congress, Jackson vetoed the Bank bill. The Bank's head, Nicholas Biddle, was a wealthy, well-educated, aristocratic Philadelphia lawyer who represented everything Jackson loathed. Biddle tried to get Congress to override Jackson's veto, but the President prevailed. Biddle managed to get the state of Pennsylvania to recharter the Bank as a private corporation.

Jackson ordered his Secretary of the Treasury to withdraw federal funds deposited with the Bank. The Secretary refused because he disagreed with Jackson's veto, and the President fired him. Jackson appointed a new Secretary of the Treasury, but the new man defied him, too, and Jackson fired him.

Finally, Jackson named Roger B. Taney of Maryland as his third Secretary of the Treasury, and Taney did the President's bidding. The Bank could not survive this blow and closed its doors. The economy was also battered by Jackson's "Bank War." Meanwhile, Jackson rewarded Taney several times over for his loyalty, ultimately naming him to succeed the late John Marshall in 1835 as the nation's fifth Chief Justice.

President Jackson considered Indians to be his personal enemies. When the state of Georgia and greedy land speculators conspired to seize the lands of the Cherokee, the most

Andrew Jackson, the seventh President (1829–1837), plunged the Presidency into the thick of party politics. The hero of the Battle of New Orleans (1815) was the target in 1835 of the first known attempt to assassinate a President. Richard Lawrence's pistols misfired at point-blank range. Jackson was not injured and had to be restrained from beating the crazed house painter to death.

"civilized" tribe by white standards, the law-abiding Cherokee invoked the protection of treaties and federal law. Chief Justice John Marshall spoke for the Supreme Court, ruling in their favor. But the President ignored the decision, and the state of Georgia ousted the Cherokee from their ancestral lands. Eventually, the Indians were forced by the Army to march under armed guard 1,000 miles west to the Oklahoma territory—a journey they called the "Trail of Tears."

President Jackson was committed to enforcing the authority of the United States against state challenges. The tariff crisis that bridged his first and second terms provided an opportunity for him to enforce federal power. The federal government had adopted a tax on imported goods, or *tariff*, which outraged the people of South Carolina, who relied on inexpensive imported goods. The state's legislature declared the tariff to be null and void (without legal force) within the state's borders.

South Carolina's action revived an issue as old as the Constitution itself—the relationship between federal power and state *sovereignty*. Advocates of state sovereignty argued that the Constitution was the creation of the several states and that the federal government was the creature of those states. Federal policy could not outweigh a state's right and duty to protect its vital interests. Thomas Jefferson and John C. Calhoun were the principal advocates of this view. But other politicians disagreed. Men such as George Washington, Alexander Hamilton, John Marshall, and Daniel Webster argued that the Constitution had been created by the people of the United States. The federal government was supreme over the states, and no state could resist the authority of the federal government.

President Jackson was ready to resist any attempt by South Carolina to defy federal authority. His first Vice President, John C. Calhoun, had resigned to go back to his native state; he returned to Washington, D.C., as a Senator from South

Carolina to lead the cause of state sovereignty against the "Tariff of Abominations."

Jackson issued a fire-breathing message to the Union and the people of South Carolina. The state legislature rejected this warning. Jackson was prepared to send the federal army to enforce the tariff in South Carolina. Finally, Senator Henry Clay of Kentucky came forward with a compromise. If the tariff were amended to take account of the needs of South Carolina, then the state would give up its opposition. Both sides accepted the compromise with relief. But the shadow of the tariff crisis would not go away. Someday a state might carry out a threat to secede from the Union, and this possibility hung over the land.

Andrew Jackson always behaved as if his will alone would determine what was law and what was government policy. He did not abide by the pattern of cooperative, nonpartisan leadership established by the first six Presidents. He challenged whatever authority tried to stand in his way. He used his veto power to reject bills that he disagreed with, departing from his predecessors' use of the veto only to reject bills they believed to be unconstitutional. When he retired after two terms, in 1836, he handpicked his successor, Martin Van Buren, his second Vice President. Van Buren, leading the Democrats, defeated the new opposition party, the Whigs.

Van Buren, a New Yorker, was the first President to be born after the Declaration of Independence. He tried to continue Jackson's policies but immediately ran into trouble. The problem was a legacy from his predecessor. Jackson had issued an executive order that federal lands could be paid for only in hard cash (gold and silver) rather than in bank notes (paper money) issued by state-chartered banks. Jackson intended his "Specie Circular" to curb free-wheeling banks that behaved as though they had an unlimited license to print money. But this gusher of paper money fueled real-estate speculation throughout the nation. The Specie Circular thus set off the

Panic of 1837, the worst economic slump the country had ever faced. President Van Buren was blamed for the Panic. His opponents turned Jacksonian ideas of equality against him, charging that Van Buren dined in the Executive Mansion with silver knives and forks from plates of gold.

The Whig Party took its name from the eighteenth-century British political party that had supported the Americans during the Revolution. In 1840, it had a Presidential candidate in the tradition of Andrew Jackson—General William Henry Harrison. Harrison had defeated the dreaded Indian leader Tecumseh at the Battle of Tippecanoe in Indiana. He was backed by a well-organized political machine with voters joining Tippecanoe clubs, and there were slogans and even a media event: The Whigs built a gigantic ball of paper and rolled it across the nation as a symbol of Harrison's momentum. Their slogans "Keep the ball rolling" and "Tippecanoe and Tyler too" entered the American language.

A Democratic editor snidely denounced Harrison, claiming that the general would be content with a jug of hard cider that he could drink on the front porch of his log cabin. The Whigs instantly seized on both symbols, hammering home the contrast between the "aristocrat" Van Buren and the unpretentious Harrison. In fact, Harrison was a Virginia aristocrat who had resettled in Ohio, in those days a western state. His handsome mansion was hardly a log cabin. But facts were scarce in the 1840 campaign, as were ideas. In fact, Whig political strategists kept Harrison at home, in the first "front porch" campaign. In addition, they rarely let Harrison make policy statements; instead, they formed a committee to draft vague, reassuring letters answering questions from voters for him to sign. Nobody was really sure what Harrison stood for, but it did not matter very much. He was elected triumphantly.

The sixty-eight-year-old Harrison was just as stubborn in his own way as Andrew Jackson had been. He insisted on delivering his ninety-minute inaugural address, on March 4, 1841, despite the cold and rainy weather; then, bare-headed, he led the Inaugural Parade on horseback. He also insisted on doing his own shopping. Within two weeks of his inauguration, he had caught a cold; within four weeks, he was dead of pneumonia, the first President to die in office.

Suddenly the all-but-forgotten Vice President, John Tyler of Virginia, was ensconced in the White House. Tyler set the precedent that when the President dies or resigns, the Vice President becomes President. The matter was not settled by the text of the Constitution; some authorities argued that only the powers and duties of the office, not the office itself, went to the Vice President when a President died or otherwise left office. In 1967, the Twenty-Fifth Amendment wrote Tyler's view into the Constitution. (The office of Vice President had been first discussed in the next-to-last week of the nearly four-month Federal Convention in 1787. Only four states had a Vice President or a Lieutenant Governor. The second highest political office in the land has been vacant sixteen times, for a total of thirty-seven years.)

Tyler was a stubborn man, and he disagreed with his own party's domestic policy, which favored federal power to build roads and canals and other "internal improvements." He used his veto power with zest, and the Whigs decided to dump him in 1844.

The Whigs' 1844 Presidential candidate, Henry Clay, lost to the Democratic nominee, James K. Polk of Tennessee, who had the unexpected support of John Tyler. Polk had been an unexpected nominee—the first *dark horse*. Polk's Presidency was dominated by the first major American war in thirty years.

In the 1820s, Americans had begun to settle in Texas, which was part of Mexico. In 1836, they revolted against Mexican rule, creating the Republic of Texas under the leadership of Sam Houston, a former governor of Tennessee and a commander of the Texas army. In 1845, the Texan Republic ended nine years of independence by joining the union as the twenty-eighth state. Texans and other Americans in the South and the West had designs on more Mexican territory. In early 1846, President Polk informed Congress that a detachment of American soldiers had been attacked by Mexican soldiers on American soil. Congress declared war, but some Whig Senators and Representatives had questions about the incident. Representative Abraham Lincoln of Illinois demanded that Polk point out the exact spot on American soil where Mexican soldiers had shed American blood.

The Mexican War was a slugfest in which Mexico found itself hopelessly outclassed. The Whigs denounced the war as a land grab designed to distract the nation from more pressing problems. Opponents of slavery charged that the war was intended to win more territory to create more slave states. By early 1848, Presidential envoy Nicholas Trist, who had studied law with Thomas Jefferson, had negotiated the Treaty of Guadalupe Hidalgo. Mexico was forced to give up about half its territory to the United States in exchange for $15 million. This territory included the present-day states of California, New Mexico, Arizona, Colorado, Utah, and Nevada. President Polk had repudiated Trist but could not quarrel with the treaty he had negotiated, and Congress quickly adopted it. Polk had promised not to run for a second term and indeed stepped down. He stunned the nation by dying four months after his retirement in March 1849.

Although the Whigs had opposed the Mexican War, they were willing to profit by it. They picked a hero of that war, General Zachary Taylor, as their 1848 Presidential candidate, to run against Democrat Lewis Cass. Taylor was elected, but in July 1850, less than halfway through his term, the old general succumbed to a stroke four days after laying the cornerstone of the Washington Monument. His successor, Vice President Millard Fillmore of New York, was another little-known politician who had been picked to balance the ticket. Fillmore helped to avert a major crisis between North and South by working with Senator Clay to put together a compromise package governing where slavery would be permitted or prohibited in the new territories. He also sent a naval expedition under Commodore Matthew C. Perry to "open" Japan to American trade and diplomatic relations. But Fillmore had little support in the Whig Party and was not nominated in 1852 for a term of his own.

The 1852 election resulted in another Democratic victory. Franklin Pierce of New Hampshire defeated another Whig Mexican War hero, General Winfield Scott. Pierce was a weak President who worked hand-in-glove with proslavery Southern Democrats. By this point, antislavery sentiment was beginning to organize for political action. In 1848, the antislavery Free Soil Party had nominated former President Martin Van Buren, and he had done surprisingly well in the race with General Taylor and Lewis Cass. The party did not do so well in 1852, but its members joined with survivors of the disintegrating Whig Party and other groups to forge a new political organization.

The Republican Party was born in 1856, taking its name from the party founded over sixty years earlier by Thomas Jefferson and James Madison. The Republicans opposed the expansion of slavery beyond those states where it was already strong. Radical members of the party wanted to do away with slavery altogether but did not press the issue. The Republicans' first Presidential candidate was the flamboyant, erratic General John C. Frémont, a noted explorer (the "Pathfinder") and military hero; he had captured Los Angeles during the Mexican War. Frémont lost to the Democratic candidate, James Buchanan of Pennsylvania, but Frémont's campaign showed that the Republicans would be a permanent force in American politics.

The new President was, at least on paper, one of the most

experienced men ever elected to the office. He had been a diplomat (Minister to Great Britain) and a long-time legislator in Washington and President Polk's Secretary of State. He was also bumbling, indecisive, and given to telling everyone what they wanted to hear. Like President Pierce, he was a "doughface"—a Northern Democrat allied with proslavery Southern Democrats. He did nothing to try to heal the splits in his party between Northern and Southern Democrats and wrung his hands as tensions between North and South increased.

In 1857, as Buchanan took office, he announced that the Supreme Court was about to settle the issues of slavery once and for all and urged all Americans to abide by the Court's decision. Chief Justice Roger B. Taney had leaked to Buchanan the substance of the Court's impending decision in *Dred Scott v. Sandford*. In that case, Chief Justice Taney ruled that slavery was protected by the Constitution and that any attempt to reach a compromise to control its spread was a violation of the Constitution. Opponents of slavery were furious. They denounced the Court and the President. Buchanan's authority and prestige faded away.

In the election of 1860, the Democrats shattered into three factions. Moderates, led by the "Little Giant," Senator Stephen A. Douglas of Illinois, stood for the principle that the people of each state should be able to vote for or against slavery. At the same time, they urged all Americans to obey the Supreme Court's decision in the *Dred Scott* case, though these two ideas were inconsistent. Proslavery Democrats endorsed Senator John C. Breckinridge of Kentucky. Those Democrats who thought it still might be possible to cobble together a compromise between North and South founded the short-lived Constitutional Union Party and put up John Bell of Tennessee.

The Republicans chose former Representative Abraham Lincoln of Illinois as their candidate. Lincoln had garnered a national reputation two years earlier when he unsuccessfully challenged Stephen Douglas in a Senate election in Illinois. The two men had debated the issues of slavery throughout the state, and the encounters received national publicity. Lincoln was a prosperous corporation and railroad lawyer, and he had argued cases before the U.S. Supreme Court; he owned one of the finest houses in Springfield, Illinois. But his supporters depicted him as a humble "rail-splitter," dubbing him "Honest Abe" (though he hated the nickname). The three-way Democratic split all but guaranteed that Lincoln would become the sixteenth President. On Election Day 1860, Lincoln indeed prevailed—with only forty percent of the popular vote.

Lincoln's victory shocked the South. Angry politicians claimed that Lincoln was the enemy of the South. His election made it impossible for the Southern states to remain in the Union. As Lincoln's inauguration approached, South Carolina, Mississippi, Florida, Alabama, Georgia, Louisiana, and Texas adopted formal declarations that they were leaving the Union. Four more states—Virginia, Arkansas, Tennessee, and North Carolina—warned that they would use force to oppose federal efforts to block any state's attempt to secede.

Buchanan declared lamely that secession would violate the Constitution—but that the United States lacked the constitutional power to prevent a state from leaving the Union. Most Americans turned away from Buchanan in disgust and waited to see what the new President would do.

CHAPTER FOUR
ABRAHAM LINCOLN

The tall, thin man from Illinois who traveled east to assume the Presidency in early 1861 was an unknown quantity to most Americans. But everyone knew that he faced the most difficult task confronting any President since George Washington. Secession, so long the "doomsday machine" of American constitutionalism, had become a reality. President Buchanan was powerless and, in fact, was predicting that he would be the last President of the United States. Most of the nation's leading military officers had resigned their commands in the U.S. Army to return home to stand with the South.

Lincoln did not believe that the Southern states would carry out their threat to leave the Union. The federal government had to stand firm. In his inaugural address, he made it clear that he would not disturb slavery where it existed but that he was unalterably opposed to its expansion. He warned the South against secession: "In *your* hands, my dissatisfied fellow-countrymen, and not in *mine*, is the momentous issue of civil war. The Government will not assail *you*. You can have no conflict without being yourselves the aggressors. *You have no oath registered in heaven to destroy the Government,* while *I* shall have the most solemn one to 'preserve, protect, and defend it.' "

The Southern states ignored the President. Virginia, Tennessee, North Carolina, and Arkansas joined the seven states that had already seceded. The eleven states held a convention in Montgomery, Alabama, and declared themselves "the Confederate States of America." They adopted a constitution modeled on the U.S. Constitution and elected Jefferson Davis of Mississippi, a former Senator and Secretary of War, as their first President. The Confederates then issued demands to Lincoln: The United States must evacuate federal military posts throughout the South. Lincoln refused.

In April 1861, Northerners and Southerners alike focused on Fort Sumter, in the harbor of Charleston, South Carolina. Lincoln vowed to resupply the federal garrison there. On the morning of April 12, Virginia-born Edmund Ruffin, a fierce, fire-eating partisan of slavery and secession, was given the honor (as he called it) of firing the first shot of the Civil War. The federal soldiers surrendered only after Confederate cannon had spent nearly a day pulverizing the fort's walls.

Lincoln issued a call for federal volunteers and ordered Congress to convene on July 4, 1861. He declared that the Confederates were a conspiracy to commit treason against the United States and refused to recognize them as a lawful government. To the President, and to most other Northerners, the conflict was "the War of the Rebellion." Southerners called it "the War Between the States" or the "Second War for Independence." Historians call it the Civil War.

Neither side expected the Civil War to last for long. They reasoned that after one good battle, the losing side would quickly sue for peace. Instead, the war lasted for four years and cost more than 600,000 American lives, North and South—more than in any other war in American history.

The war did not start out as a war over slavery. It was a struggle between two different views of the Constitution and the Union. President Lincoln was the latest of a long line of politicians and theorists going back to George Washington and Alexander Hamilton who had argued that the Constitution and the Union were created by the American people and were thus supreme over the states. Jefferson Davis was the latest spokesman of the "state compact" or "state sovereignty" theory of the Constitution most often associated with Thomas Jefferson and John C. Calhoun. Reason and argument and compromise had not decided the issue—now it would be resolved by force of arms.

The war forced Lincoln to change the way that the Presidency fit into the constitutional system. Because the United States was at war to preserve the Constitution and the Union, the President could no longer just carry out policies decided by Congress. He had to make policy as well, as part of his responsibility as Commander-in-Chief under the Constitution. President Lincoln seized the opportunity to resolve the crisis of the Union through the authority of the Presidency.

Some critics of Lincoln and his Administration charged that the President was setting himself up as a dictator. One of his measures provoked particular alarm. An important cornerstone of our legal system is that the government cannot arrest and detain anyone it wants to. It must have reasons, and those reasons must be authorized by law. Any person held by a government official may apply to a court for a special document called a *writ of habeas corpus*. This writ compels the government official to bring the prisoner before the court and explain the valid reasons for holding the prisoner in custody. If the court rejects these reasons, the prisoner must go free. The Constitution permits the government to suspend the writ in extreme circumstances. Lincoln issued an order suspending the writ, even though critics argued—with some reason—that only Congress could take that action; later, Congress passed a law ratifying Lincoln's order.

Lincoln recognized that the effort to preserve the Union was endangering individuals' civil liberties. He justified his measures by saying that, even if he had violated the letter of the Constitution, he had done so to save the Constitution. Should he let the entire Constitution fall because he might violate a part of it? To Lincoln, the answer was clear. Jefferson Davis and his colleagues took similar steps in the South.

Throughout the war, Lincoln was a vigorous Commander-in-Chief, frequently urging particular strategies and tactics on his generals. He appointed and supported the best generals he could find and fired and replaced them when he believed that they were not effective or determined enough to achieve victory. In 1862, at the Battle of Norfolk, Virginia, the President was so exasperated by one general's failure to move against Confederate forces that he actually took the field himself and directed Union soldiers to victory. Many generals who had spent their lives in uniform resented this civilian who had been only a volunteer captain in the Illinois militia in skirmishes against the Indians thirty years earlier.

The Civil War reached into Lincoln's family. Several relatives of his wife, Mary Todd Lincoln, fought for the South. At one point, President Lincoln appeared before a secret session of a Congressional committee investigating his wife's loyalty to assure them that his wife was not a rebel agent. The problems of the Lincolns and the Todds were examples of conflicts afflicting many other families throughout the United States.

At one point during the Civil War, the United States was nearly plunged into a war with Great Britain. A Union ship seized two Confederate envoys bound for Great Britain on a British ship. After Queen Victoria's husband, Prince Albert, and President Lincoln intervened, the envoys were released, and war between Great Britain and the United States averted. The Confederate envoys failed in their attempt to forge an alliance with the British, and the Confederacy never managed to find a foreign ally to support their struggle.

At first, the strategy of the war was dictated by assumptions that had been adopted fifty years earlier, during the European Napoleonic Wars. The object of each side was to capture the enemy capital. Thus, Lincoln sought a general who could capture Richmond, Virginia, the Confederate capital, and Robert E. Lee, the leading Confederate general, tried time and time again to encircle and conquer Washington, D.C. But Lincoln eventually realized that the Civil War was the first example of a new kind of war—one of populations and resources and technology. The old, chess-like strategies of war were no longer relevant. The Civil War was the first total war.

As the war dragged on, Lincoln was more and more willing to revise the war's aims. He knew that declaring that the war's goals were to crush slavery as well as to preserve the Union would win the Union cause increased popularity in the North, and in Europe as well. In the summer of 1862, he drafted a proclamation freeing the slaves in the Confederate states, but his Cabinet persuaded him to wait for an appropriate time to release it. A Union victory on the battlefield would be best, they cautioned. And so the President waited until the Union triumph in the Battle of Antietam in Maryland. In one of the bloodiest contests of the whole war, the Confederate forces under General Robert E. Lee were forced back across the Potomac River. This was enough of a victory for Lincoln. The date was September 17, 1862, the seventy-fifth anniversary of the signing of the U.S. Constitution.

The Emancipation Proclamation was carefully crafted not to offend slaveholders in states remaining loyal to the Union. It freed all slaves in areas *still in rebellion* against the United States, a clause that exempted areas already under federal military control. It offered slaveholding rebels a choice: Submit to the Union and your slaves may not be freed, or persist in your rebellion at the risk that, if you lose, you will lose everything. The Proclamation had great symbolic value, and when Union armies conquered Southern territory, they freed the slaves they found there.

Lincoln and Congress wrestled over the conduct of the war. Congress established the Joint Committee on the Conduct of the War, which aided Lincoln by exposing corruption and mismanagement but also tried to dictate strategy and policies to be pursued in the defeated Confederacy. In matters pertaining to the war, Lincoln insisted on his constitutional authority as Commander-in-Chief. In other matters,

Abraham Lincoln, the sixteenth President (1861–1865), ranks with George Washington as one of the two greatest Presidents. His aim during the Civil War was to preserve the Constitution at all costs. Once it became clear that the United States would win, he also declared the war to be a war against slavery. He was the first of four Presidents who have been assassinated.

Lincoln deferred to Congress or cooperated with Congressional leaders.

Lincoln's Cabinet was a mixed blessing. It included men of unquestioned ability, such as his former rival Secretary of State William Seward, and corrupt hacks, such as Secretary of War Simon Cameron. Lincoln was saddled with Cameron, who had been the Republican "boss" of Pennsylvania, as the result of a political deal at the 1860 Republican convention. Thanks to the investigations of the Joint Committee on the Conduct of the War, Lincoln was able to transfer Cameron to the harmless job of American Minister to Russia. He replaced him with a tough-minded War Democrat, Edwin M. Stanton, who cured the Department's corruption, improved its efficiency, and placed it squarely behind the war effort. When Lincoln finally settled on General Ulysses S. Grant as the Union commander in the field, the President, Stanton, and Grant functioned as a smoothly working, winning team.

The Presidential election of 1864 was the most unusual in our history, as it was carried on while the nation was torn apart by war. Lincoln believed that it was vital to demonstrate to the American people and the rest of the world that the orderly processes of government continued despite the rebellion. Republicans and War Democrats joined forces for this election as the National Union Party; their candidates were President Lincoln and Andrew Johnson of Tennessee, the only Southern Senator not to walk out of Congress. The Democratic Party nominated General George B. McClellan, formerly commander of the Union Army of the Potomac. McClellan had championed intensive military buildups but was overly cautious about using these forces against the Confederates; he was denied any field command after failing to pursue General Lee's retreating Confederates from Antietam. He ran as a peace candidate, hoping that his popularity among Union soldiers might bring him enough votes for victory. The Democrats also hoped that their choice of a war hero idolized by the rank-and-file soldiers of the Union would dispel public doubts about their patriotism.

Lincoln feared that he might not be re-elected. To lay the groundwork for a peaceful transfer of power, he had his Cabinet sign a folded piece of paper without telling them what he had written on it. It was a mass letter of resignation, which Lincoln would accept as the first step for preparing the transition to a McClellan administration. It proved unnecessary. Lincoln defeated McClellan by a margin large enough to give him a mandate for his war policy.

Photographs of Lincoln made as he began his second term show a worn, exhausted man carrying on his conscience every death, Union and Confederate, caused by the war. The early months of 1865 brought news that the war was finally coming to an end. General Grant was hemming in the remnants of Lee's Army of Northern Virginia; General William T. Sherman's campaign of fire and devastation in Georgia and South Carolina was pulverizing Southern resistance. The President's Second Inaugural Address, delivered on March 4, sketched his hopes for the society that would emerge from the war:

> With malice toward none, with charity for all, with firmness in the right as God gives us to see the right, let us strive to finish the work we are in, to bind up the nation's wounds, to care for him who shall have borne the battle and for his widow and his orphan, to do all which may achieve a just and lasting peace among ourselves and with all nations.

Grant's strategy of wearing Lee down had paid off. Within four weeks of Lincoln's inauguration, Richmond, the Confederate capital, had fallen. On April 9, 1865, General Grant accepted General Lee's surrender at Appomattox Courthouse, Virginia. (The white flags of truce, actually a towel and a pair of underdrawers, were accepted by Major General George A. Custer, who would enter the history books again at the Battle of Little Bighorn, in 1876.) The "Confederate States of America" was dead; the Union was secure. When he heard the news of the fall of the Confederacy, old Edmund Ruffin, who had fired the first shot of the war and had enlisted with rebel forces as a symbolic gesture, committed suicide by placing a silver-mounted rifle in his mouth and pulling the trigger.

President Lincoln had only five days to savor the Union's victory and the adulation of his countrymen. After four years of vilification and criticism, the President was now the most popular man in America. On Good Friday, April 14, he chose to relax by attending a popular British comedy, *Our American Cousin*, at Ford's Theatre in Washington, D.C. As Lincoln and his party sat in the Presidential box laughing at the play, a twenty-six-year-old actor named John Wilkes Booth slipped past a negligent security guard, crept up behind the President, and fired a bullet into his brain. Lincoln never regained consciousness; he died the next day. Secretary Stanton said at the moment of Lincoln's death, "Now he belongs to the ages." It was the first murder of a President in American history.

Booth was a rabid Southern sympathizer. He had continued his acting career in Northern theaters during the war but burned to do something for the rebel cause. In early 1865, he had spun a mad plot to kidnap the President and hold him hostage for the Confederacy's independence. He changed his mind, however, and assembled a gang of third-rate thugs, criminals, and hangers-on to murder every high official of the Administration. Booth would deal with Lincoln himself. Another conspirator, assigned to murder Vice President Johnson, lost his nerve. Still another stabbed Secretary of State Seward, but Seward survived the attack.

Secretary of War Stanton took charge in the hours after

Lincoln's murder. Union soldiers cornered Booth in a barn a few miles from the capital. A deranged private, Boston Corbett, shot Booth dead, acting (he claimed) on orders from God. The other conspirators were swiftly arrested, tried, convicted, and hanged.

Lincoln's funeral was the occasion for a national outpouring of grief. Even former rebels expressed sorrow. They were also fearful. They were not sure what fate the vengeful Johnson Administration would mete out to the defeated South.

Lincoln had hoped for a peaceful retirement in Springfield, where he might practice law and write his memoirs. Fate denied that wish, but his memory lives. He ranks with Washington as one of the two greatest Presidents, and many would agree that he is our most beloved historical figure.

CHAPTER FIVE

FROM FORD'S THEATRE TO EXPOSITION HALL

In 1865, President Abraham Lincoln was shot dead. In 1901, President William McKinley was mortally wounded by the gunfire of another assassin. These two gunshots, both at point-blank range, marked the beginning and the end of an era in the history of the Presidency. In this thirty-six-year period, most Americans believed that the Presidency should subside into its "normal" role of carrying out the will of Congress. In his classic work *The American Commonwealth,* which first appeared in 1888, the Scottish historian and diplomat James Bryce devoted a chapter to the question "Why Great Men Are Not Chosen President." Trying to explain why such ciphers as W. H. Harrison, James Buchanan, and Franklin Pierce had become President while such great men as Henry Clay, John C. Calhoun, and Daniel Webster had not, Bryce suggested that the office provided no room for great men to do great things.

Lincoln's successor, Andrew Johnson, helped to bring about the situation that Bryce described, for he nearly brought the Presidency to disaster. At first, Johnson shared the desire of "Radical" Republicans in Congress to punish the

Southern states for their rebellion, for Lincoln's murder, and for the pain and suffering left by the Civil War. But Johnson did not have a strong commitment to racial equality and to helping the freed slaves, as Lincoln and the Republicans had. He was willing to restore the conditions of Southern political life to what they had been before the war—with the whites safely in charge. But the Republicans who controlled Congress believed that it would be too dangerous for the nation to allow the politicians who had ruled the South in the years before the war to resume their power.

Congress framed a policy to govern the defeated Southern states as conquered territories and to protect the civil rights of freed slaves and other black Americans. This policy was called *Reconstruction*. President Johnson bitterly opposed Reconstruction and used his veto power to prevent Reconstruction bills from becoming law. Congress overrode Johnson's vetoes, but the President stubbornly refused to carry out the laws. This contest over Reconstruction policy escalated into a showdown between the President and the Congress.

The flashpoint came when Congress, fearing that the President would fire Cabinet members who agreed with Reconstruction, enacted over Johnson's veto a law known as the Tenure of Office Act: If the President wanted to fire any official whose appointment had required the consent of the Senate, he had to get Senate authorization to fire the official. Johnson tried to fire Secretary of War Edwin Stanton, but when the Senate refused its permission, the President defied the Senate and fired Stanton anyway. The Secretary of War barricaded himself in his office at the War Department and sent word to Congress.

Congress saw a chance to get rid of Johnson once and for all. The angry House of Representatives declared that the President had committed "high Crimes and Misdemeanors" justifying his removal from office through the constitutional process of impeachment. The Representatives did not care that Johnson had only a year left in his term of office. With remarkable speed, the House voted to impeach Johnson for violating the Tenure of Office Act. They framed eleven articles of impeachment and sent these formal charges to the Senate for trial.

The spring of 1868 was dominated by the first Presidential impeachment in American history. The President's defenders claimed that he could not be removed from office unless the House and Senate could show that he had committed specific violations of law, such as murder or fraud, for which a person could be indicted by a grand jury. Johnson's accusers replied that an impeachable offense was something more than a violation of criminal law. It could be whatever a majority of the House and two-thirds of the Senate thought it to be—or, at the least, a severe political offense against the Constitution and laws.

As required by the Constitution, the Chief Justice of the United States, Salmon P. Chase, presided over the Senate's trial of the President on the charges brought by the House. Chase worked hard to make certain that the Senate's trial would be fair and impartial. He did not want the process to degenerate into a political lynching.

Due to the Chief Justice's efforts, the supporters of impeachment began to worry that their campaign to oust the President might fail. They calculated that one-third of the Senators would vote to acquit the President. One more vote would save him, for the Constitution requires a two-thirds vote by the Senate for conviction and removal from office. As the roll call proceeded, Senator Edmund G. Ross of Kansas quietly waited for his name to be called. He was a Radical Republican who favored Congressional Reconstruction and often had voted against Johnson's vetoes, but he had his doubts about the impeachment effort. The pro-impeachment forces had counted him among their ranks, but when the clerk of the Senate called Ross's name, the Senator answered firmly: "Not Guilty." He had saved Johnson and the Presidency—and destroyed his own political career.

Historians agree that if Johnson had been convicted, the independence of the Presidency would have been destroyed. Congress would have had the power to oust a President simply for disagreeing with it rather than for the serious reasons that an impeachment requires. Nonetheless, the impeachment effort left a deep scar on the Presidency. For the rest of the century, Johnson's successors had to defend the office from the encroachments of Congress.

Johnson's successor, General Ulysses S. Grant, made peace with Congress—but on Congress's terms. The victorious Union general was a national hero, and the Republicans believed that he would be their ideal candidate in the 1868 election. Grant indeed triumphed in 1868, and won reelection in 1872, as the symbol of the common man. Unfortunately, in office he turned out to be all too common. Congress quickly let him know who was really running the government, and Grant gave in. All that can be said in favor of Grant's Presidency is that he was the first President since Andrew Jackson, four decades earlier, to serve two full terms of office. Grant went along with Congressional Reconstruction but did little to protect the rights of freed slaves. His Administration was notable mainly for its epidemic of corruption at almost every level of government. When he left office in 1876, the nation breathed a collective sigh of relief. Americans wanted to remember Grant as the military leader who had triumphed over the Confederate armies, not as the symbol of American political corruption.

The 1876 Presidential election was a paradox: It was the dirtiest campaign in our history, and yet it featured two of the cleanest Presidential candidates in American history. Republican Rutherford B. Hayes, the Governor of Ohio and a former Union general, squared off against Democrat Samuel J. Tilden, the Governor of New York. At first, it seemed that

Tilden, with fifty-one percent of the popular vote, had been elected. Hayes even conceded defeat to a reporter. But Republicans swiftly charged that vote fraud in three Southern states—Louisiana, Florida, and South Carolina—had cost Hayes the election. As the Constitution provides, the disputed election went into the House of Representatives, but Congress decided instead to name a special investigating commission to weigh the claims of each candidate to the disputed electoral votes. Tilden needed only one of these nineteen electoral votes to win the election, but Hayes needed all nineteen of them. After a still-mysterious series of deals and trades, the commission awarded the Republican Hayes all the electoral votes of the disputed states. In return, Republicans in Congress pledged to end Reconstruction and withdraw the federal soldiers who occupied the Southern states.

President Hayes was an honest man who was the prisoner of the Republican Party organization; all he could do was close his eyes to the wheeling and dealing that put him into the Executive Mansion. He complied with the pledges made by the Republicans in Congress, ordering the withdrawal of the occupying army from the former Confederate states. North and South tried to pretend that the Civil War was behind them. Hayes's great cause was civil service reform. He fought for laws to establish qualifications for government jobs and a system of merit selection to make sure that only the best qualified persons could win office. His integrity was widely respected, but the Republican Party organization was not willing to renominate him in 1880. (Mrs. Hayes, a temperance advocate nicknamed "Lemonade Lucy," was the first President's wife to be called the First Lady.)

Both the Republicans and the Democrats now resorted to nominating Civil War generals for the Presidency. The Democrats chose Winfield Scott Hancock, nicknamed "Superb" for his valiant stands in battle. The Republicans resisted the blandishments of former President Grant, seeking a chance for an unprecedented third term at the urging of Senator Roscoe Conkling of New York. They settled on a compromise ticket. Their candidate was Representative James A. Garfield of Ohio (a former general of the Union's Army of the Cumberland). The Republicans were split into two great factions, the Stalwarts (party loyalists who resisted such reforms as civil service) and the Mugwumps (who accepted these reforms). Garfield was a Mugwump, and his running mate, Chester A. Arthur of New York, was a Stalwart and a Conkling protégé. The Republicans narrowly defeated the Democrats in a dull campaign.

Garfield was a polished orator, but he was a weak man who bent to the pressure of the party bosses. He found no joy in the Presidency, but he did not last long. In the summer of 1881, after only four months in office, he was walking with Secretary of State James G. Blaine through the waiting room of the Baltimore and Potomac railroad station in Washington, D.C., when thirty-nine-year-old Charles J. Guiteau shot him twice in the back at point-blank range. Crying out, "My God, what is this?" Garfield fell to the floor as bystanders disarmed Guiteau. The assassin surrendered without a fight. "I am a Stalwart, and Arthur is President!" he shouted confidently. The mentally unstable Guiteau had made a nuisance of himself demanding a government job for having supported Garfield, who had ignored his requests. But Guiteau was not given a political reward. Instead, he was arrested and jailed. His lawyers tried to persuade the court that Guiteau was insane, but he refused to permit the tactic. He told the court that God had ordered him to kill the President. He was convicted, sentenced to death, and—singing "I am going to the Lord, I am so glad"—hanged. President Garfield lingered in agony for more than two months before dying on September 19.

Speculation swirled around the elegant, easy-going Chester

A. Arthur. In the 1870s, he had been Collector of Customs at the Port of New York, a job he owed to Senator Conkling, and in that post had turned a blind eye to the rampant corruption flourishing there. Once he became President, however, Arthur amazed all who had known him: He became an even more ardent opponent of corruption and champion of civil service than Hayes had been. Arthur was not considered for nomination in 1884. As it happened, Arthur was suffering from Bright's disease, a fatal kidney ailment, and he died less than two years after leaving office.

The 1884 Presidential election was another lively—and dirty—campaign. The Democratic candidate, Governor Grover Cleveland of New York, seemed incorruptible—until a young woman came forward and accused him of being the father of her illegitimate son. The unmarried Cleveland admitted that her charges were plausible and promised to assume responsibility for the child. His opponent, the handsome and articulate James G. Blaine of Maine, was nicknamed the "Plumed Knight" by his adoring supporters. But Blaine turned out to have been mired in several of the worst scandals of the Grant era.

One anonymous editor suggested that Cleveland's public career was honorable but that his private life was stained; Blaine's private life was above reproach, but his public record was open to question. Therefore, the voters should choose Cleveland for the Presidency and retire Blaine to private life. The voters did prefer Cleveland, but the Democrat's victory was due mostly to a joke made by a Republican clergyman who denounced the Democrats as "the party of Rum, Romanism, and Rebellion!" Democratic strategists made sure that every Roman Catholic voter heard about the slur in time for the election.

Cleveland was the most vigorous defender of the Presidency in this period. He became known as the "veto President" because of his 301 vetoes in his first term (and 584 in his two terms). Most of these vetoes rejected "private pension bills" to benefit veterans of the Civil War; Cleveland showed, in veto messages dripping with sarcasm, that the vetoed claims for pensions were completely unjustified. His four years in office resulted in a budget surplus of $100 million.

Cleveland is the only President to be married in the Executive Mansion. The forty-nine-year-old President married his twenty-one-year-old ward in a wedding that was the social event of the year. John Philip Sousa and the Marine Band provided the music. Mrs. Cleveland won the hearts of the nation—and boosted her husband's popularity.

The Democrats cheerfully renominated the President in 1888. Against him, the Republicans pitted yet another Civil War general, Benjamin Harrison of Indiana, a hero in the Atlanta campaign. Harrison was the grandson of the ninth President, William Henry Harrison, and the Republicans made much of the family relationship (though "Tippecanoe" had served only one month). The principal issue of the election was whether, as the Republicans argued, the nation should adopt tariffs to protect American industries from foreign competition or whether it should continue its policy of *free trade*, allowing the forces of the market to determine prices and requiring American manufacturers to compete with European manufacturers. Cleveland edged Harrison in the popular vote—but Harrison carried states with a majority of electoral votes and became President.

In four years, the Harrison Administration managed to dissipate the surplus that the Cleveland Administration had amassed in the federal treasury. Congress abandoned free trade, but the tariffs injured American trade with Europe and led to an economic downturn. Scenting victory, the Democrats in 1892 called Cleveland out of political retirement and won back the Presidency.

The economic slump under President Harrison grew into the Depression of 1893, which cast a pall over Cleveland's second term. Other economic problems plagued the nation as well. The most serious was the Pullman strike of 1894. The Pullman Palace Car Company, a manufacturer of railroad sleeping cars, had founded what it considered to be a "model town" for its workers and had sharply reduced employee wages. Pullman workers hated Pullman, Illinois, claiming that it was little better than a prison. They struck the company, demanding better wages and the right to be paid in cash, which they could spend anywhere, rather than in "scrip" good only at the "company stores" in Pullman. The employers called for government help to quell the strike, which spread to other railroads and crippled rail traffic between Chicago and the West Coast. U.S. Attorney General Richard Olney, who was himself a railroad director, persuaded the President to send in federal soldiers to break the strike to get the U.S. mail moving. In the bloody violence that followed, the workers suffered heavy casualties.

Cleveland had troubles in foreign policy as well. He defended the Monroe Doctrine so vigorously in a boundary dispute between Venezuela and the British colony of British Guiana that the United States nearly went to war with Great Britain. The dispute eventually was peacefully resolved in favor of British Guiana.

The President suffered a grave illness in his second term and underwent an operation for cancer. Half of his upper jaw was removed and replaced with a rubber part. The operation, carried out on board a yacht in the East River in New York City, was performed in secret; not even Vice President Adlai Stevenson was informed. Not until twenty-four years later, ten years after Cleveland's death, was the operation disclosed to the public.

The farmers of the West were hit hard by the 1893 Depression and blamed their plight on Eastern bankers and politicians who kept a tight rein on the nation's money supply. The farmers claimed that the monetary system thus prevented them from being able to pay their debts. They demanded that the government issue silver money at the inflated rate of sixteen silver dollars for every gold dollar in circulation; "free silver," they thought, would make it easier for them to repay their debts. President Cleveland opposed this policy because he feared its effects on the stability of American money.

At the Democratic Convention in 1896, a thirty-six-year-old Nebraska lawyer and delegate, William Jennings Bryan, brought the delegates to their feet with an eloquent, impassioned plea for free silver. At the end of his speech, he cried, "You shall not crucify mankind upon this cross of gold!" The "Cross of Gold" speech won Bryan the Democratic Presidential nomination, though most of the delegates had never heard of him before the convention.

Bryan was the youngest man ever nominated for the Presidency by a major political party. He energetically campaigned across the nation by train, preaching the glories of free silver and denouncing the heartless Eastern financial community. By contrast, the Republican nominee, William McKinley, stayed home on his front porch in Ohio, receiving visiting delegations and making vague speeches for the newspapers. Governor McKinley, an experienced politician, was the last Presidential candidate to have served in the Civil War. He defeated Bryan and won the Presidency back for the Republicans.

Within a year of his inauguration in 1897, McKinley became a reluctant war President. The United States had long distrusted Spain and resented the few remaining Spanish colonies in the Western Hemisphere and the Pacific islands, such as Cuba, Puerto Rico, and the Philippines. They listened eagerly to exaggerated reports of Spanish atrocities and mistreatment of Cubans, Puerto Ricans, Filipinos, and foreign nationals in these colonies. In February 1898, the battleship U.S.S. *Maine,* lying at anchor in the harbor of Havana, Cuba, suddenly and mysteriously exploded and sank, killing

260 American sailors. Infuriated Americans blamed Spain. The Spanish government insisted that it had not been responsible and offered all help needed to investigate the tragedy. But the American press and the American people had made up their minds, and Congress and the President soon fell into step. McKinley explained that, after much prayer, he had decided that the United States had to go to war to free and civilize "our little brown brothers."

The Spanish-American War was a disgrace. Mark Twain denounced it as the international equivalent of bullying. In battles on land and sea, American forces easily overcame the Spanish army and navy. The United States wrested the Philippines, Cuba, Puerto Rico, and other colonies in the Pacific from the Spanish. In an unrelated incident, American settlers in the independent kingdom of Hawaii overthrew the centuries-old monarchy there and persuaded the United States to annex the islands 3,000 miles southwest of California.

William Jennings Bryan won the Democratic Presidential nomination again in 1900, this time denouncing the Spanish-American War and American "imperialism." He charged that the Republicans had conned the American people into grabbing an empire for the United States as greedily as the British, French, Germans, Belgians, and other Europeans were doing in Africa and Asia. The Republicans renominated President McKinley and chose as his new running-mate Theodore Roosevelt of New York. Roosevelt had been Assistant Secretary of the Navy in 1898, and had ordered the mobilization of the Navy immediately after the destruction of the *Maine*. He had then resigned to organize a volunteer cavalry unit, the "Rough Riders." Colonel Roosevelt became the hero of the Battle of San Juan Hill in Cuba and returned home to win the Governorship of New York. Terrified by TR's campaign for reform and efficiency in government, the New York Republican political machine successfully begged McKinley to "kick

Roosevelt upstairs," to get him out of the state and into a job where he could do no damage. The President's mentor and campaign manager, Ohio industrialist Mark Hanna, despised Roosevelt, calling him a "damn cowboy." On being nominated, Roosevelt traveled by rail across the nation as energetically as Bryan, making hundreds of speeches while President McKinley once again conducted a "front porch" campaign. Running on the theme of the "full dinner pail," which emphasized American prosperity, the Republicans again won the Presidency.

McKinley had no real enemies. He was popular with, even beloved by, the American people. In September 1901, he traveled to Buffalo, New York, to open the Pan-American Exposition taking place there. As he shook hands in a receiving line in the Exposition's Temple of Music, McKinley noticed that one guest had his right hand wrapped in a bandage. The President reached out to shake the man's hand.

Suddenly, two shots rang out from a pistol concealed under the bandage and McKinley collapsed, mortally wounded. His assassin was a twenty-eight-year-old unemployed mill worker named Leon Czolgosz, who declared that he had nothing against the President. His crime was an act of principle, Czolgosz explained in broken English; he was an *anarchist*, someone who wanted to abolish all governments. The President died after eight days, and the nation went into mourning. But Mark Hanna, who had built McKinley's political career, had special reason to mourn his friend's death and to worry about the future. "Good Lord!" he cried. "Now that Goddamn cowboy is President of the United States!"

CHAPTER SIX

THE PROGRESSIVE PRESIDENTS: THEODORE ROOSEVELT, TAFT, WILSON

Theodore Roosevelt was the first President to have an understanding of the office that we would recognize today. He was the first President to use the office to take the lead in identifying national problems and proposing solutions to them. He was the first President to believe that the President has the power and the responsibility to set the national agenda. He declared that the Presidency was a "bully pulpit"—and he made the most of it. He knew how to get his message to the people through the press. He knew how to capture the popular imagination.

No one could be neutral about Theodore Roosevelt. His youth and vigor delighted and amazed the nation. His active, rambunctious children interrupted diplomatic negotiations and formal receptions, driving wagons through the halls of the White House (a name that Roosevelt coined) and engaging their father in wrestling matches before astonished dignitaries. One observer declared: "At every wedding, Theodore wants to be the bride. At every funeral, he wants to be the corpse."

On the domestic front, Roosevelt fought to conserve America's natural resources and such natural wonders as Yosemite National Park, on the west slope of the Sierra Nevada in California. His environmental mentor was Gifford Pinchot, whom Roosevelt named to head the new National Park Service. The President also sought to control the giant corporations, the monopolies and trusts and holding companies that controlled the wealth and economic life of the nation. He became known as the "trust buster."

On the world stage, the President pursued a strong, even aggressive foreign policy. He sent the American "Great White Fleet" around the world to show off American might. When Congress had resisted the idea, refusing to appropriate money to pay for the odyssey, Roosevelt ordered the expedition anyway. The fleet had only enough fuel to go halfway around the globe; Congress was forced to appropriate funds to pay for more fuel to bring the ships home—the outcome that the President had in mind all along.

When Colombia would not permit the United States to build a canal through its narrow strip of Central American land known as Panama, Roosevelt connived with American settlers and local revolutionaries. The result was a revolution in Panama. The President bolstered the Panamanian bid for independence by parking an American gunboat offshore to protect American citizens (who were helping to lead the Revolution). When Colombia was forced to recognize Panama's independence, Roosevelt negotiated a treaty with the Panamanian government that granted the United States a perpetual lease of a ten-mile-wide strip across Panama. The United States thus got to dig the "great ditch," the Panama Canal, linking the Atlantic and Pacific oceans and eliminating the interminable ship passage around South America—the greatest engineering project of the age. Roosevelt later boasted: "I took the Canal—and let Congress debate." As the canal was being built, the President was so impatient to see the result of his maneuvering that he sailed to Panama to take a look for himself, becoming the first President to leave the continental United States while in office.

In 1904, Roosevelt ran for a term of his own. He won by a landslide, the first since President Lincoln had defeated General McClellan in 1864. His Democratic opponent was a conservative judge, Alton B. Parker of New York. Roosevelt's slogan, borrowed from the game of poker, was "Stand Pat." (Parker's running mate, Henry G. Davis of West Virginia, was, at eighty-one, the oldest major party candidate ever nominated for national office.)

Roosevelt's second term was even more successful than his first in some ways, and his greatest achievement won international praise. In 1905, the President decided to try to end the destructive and useless war between Russia and Japan. He offered his services as mediator, and the two nations sent delegations to Portsmouth, New Hampshire, where Roosevelt bullied, charmed, and reasoned them into an agreement. For his role in negotiating the Treaty of Portsmouth, Roosevelt became the first American to receive the Nobel Peace Prize.

Roosevelt announced that he would not seek another term of office. He brushed aside questions about what an energetic fifty-year-old ex-President would find to occupy himself. He endorsed as his successor his friend and Secretary of War, William Howard Taft, who easily defeated William Jennings Bryan's third, and last, bid for the Presidency. Roosevelt went off to Africa to hunt big game.

Taft was the heaviest man ever to become President. The 350-pound Ohioan had been a distinguished lawyer and judge and Governor-General of the Philippines after the Spanish-American War. His lifelong dream was to become Chief Justice, but the opportunity never presented itself. Ironically, in 1910, he appointed another man to the office he craved for himself.

Taft pursued many of the policies that Roosevelt had launched. He actually was a more vigorous trust buster than

Theodore Roosevelt loved being the twenty-sixth President (1901–1909) so much that he ran for a third term in 1912 (but lost). The Rough Rider brought boundless energy to the Presidency, making it the focus of modern American government.

Roosevelt had been. His conservation policy differed from Roosevelt's, however. His Secretary of the Interior, Richard Ballinger, tangled repeatedly with Gifford Pinchot in a bruising dispute over conservation. Roosevelt was outraged. He charged that Taft had betrayed his legacy. Rumors flew that Roosevelt was thinking of challenging Taft for the Presidency in 1912.

The Republican convention that year confirmed the rumors, but Taft beat back the Roosevelt forces. If the Republicans and the nation expected Roosevelt to take his defeat lying down, however, they were mistaken. The ex-President called for a new convention—a convention of "Progressives."

Historians identify Roosevelt as the first Progressive President. The Progressives were a wide and diverse movement of political, social, and economic reformers including Republicans and Democrats. Taft, too, was a Progressive, though not as consistent as Roosevelt. The break between the two men resulted in Taft's ouster from the Progressive movement.

The Progressive convention was a rag-tag collection of reformers and Rough Riders—and some political cranks. They organized themselves as a new political party, the Progressive Party, and nominated Roosevelt by acclamation. Roosevelt accepted the nomination, declaring, "My hat is in the ring" and "I feel as fit as a bull moose!" This defiant statement earned the Progressive Party the nickname of the Bull Moose Party. Roosevelt rallied his supporters to support the policies he dubbed "the New Nationalism," proclaiming: "We stand at Armageddon and we battle for the Lord!"

Meanwhile, the Democrats had chosen their nominee—another product of the Progressive movement, Governor Woodrow Wilson of New Jersey. Born in Virginia, Wilson was the first Southern-born candidate for the White House since Kentucky-born Abraham Lincoln in 1860. Wilson had been a lawyer, a scholar, and the president of Princeton University before the Democratic machine politicians of New Jersey picked him as a figurehead candidate for Governor. Anyone looking at Wilson's stubborn jaw should have known better. He was his own man, and he soon became known as one of the most liberal and forward-looking members of the Democratic Party.

Wilson differed from Roosevelt and Taft. They believed that not all concentrations of wealth and economic power were always bad. They maintained that government should break up such concentrations of wealth and power only when they clearly threatened the public interest. Otherwise, government should work cooperatively with business and labor. Governor Wilson agreed with his friend and ally the Boston lawyer and social critic Louis D. Brandeis that one of the greatest threats faced by the American people was the "curse of bigness." Wilson coined the phrase "New Freedom" to describe his policies.

The 1912 campaign was notable for the first attempt to assassinate a Presidential candidate. As Roosevelt was about to enter a hall in Milwaukee, Wisconsin, to make a speech, he was shot by John N. Schrank, a thirty-six-year-old German immigrant bartender who acted under the delusion that the ghost of President McKinley had ordered him to execute Roosevelt for McKinley's murder. Roosevelt was carrying a thick manuscript of his speech folded up in his breast pocket. The manuscript and the ex-President's metal eyeglass case absorbed the impact of the .32 calibre bullet, saving Roosevelt's life. Though the bullet fractured a rib, TR insisted on delivering the hour-long speech, and afterward was rushed to a hospital. (The bullet was never removed.)

In the election of 1912, the split between Taft and Roosevelt resulted in a popular vote of only 42 percent for Wilson, but he racked up a landslide (435 votes) in the Electoral College. Roosevelt outpolled Taft in both the popular and the electoral votes—the only time that a third-party candidate has outstripped a major party's nominee, and the incumbent at that.

To some extent, Roosevelt's defeat was his own fault. He had tried to defy the venerable two-term tradition. Although he argued that he had had only one term of his own, this justification of his candidacy did not convince the voters. He returned to private life, to journalism, and to the frustration of being out of the arena. Taft retired to Yale Law School to teach and write.

President Wilson's stubbornness soon got him into trouble with Congress, and he was not consistently successful in getting what he wanted from it. But he scored a major coup. He became the first President since John Adams to appear before Congress to deliver his message on the "state of the Union" rather than to send it in writing. This step confirmed the President's role in setting the agenda of national politics.

Wilson supported a stronger antitrust law to break up large businesses. He won creation of a new government agency, the Federal Reserve Board, to regulate American currency and to help stabilize the economy.

The President's first wife had died in August 1914, but in December 1915 the nation buzzed with the news that the President had fallen in love again. The new Mrs. Wilson, a widow, Edith Bolling Galt, was extremely popular with the country and the press, which gushed over the "White House romance" and made the Presidential wedding front-page news.

In 1916, the President sought a second term. His Republican opponent was Charles Evans Hughes of New York, who had stepped down from a Supreme Court Justiceship. His reformist credentials satisfied even Theodore Roosevelt (though the former President grumbled that Hughes reminded him of the bearded lady at the circus). Hughes had been a capable Governor of New York and a first-rate Justice. By accepting the Republican Presidential nomination, he united the Taft and Roosevelt wings of the party. The contest was close—so close that Hughes and Wilson both believed that Hughes had won. But Hughes had made a major mistake during the campaign. He had offended Republican Governor Hiram Johnson of California, who refused to lift a finger to help Hughes's campaign. As a result, California went for Wilson by a hair—giving the President a second term.

Wilson had campaigned on the slogan "He Kept Us Out of War." In 1914, war had erupted in Europe in the wake of the assassination of Archduke Franz Ferdinand of Austria-Hungary by a Serbian nationalist. The catastrophic struggle that we now call the First World War appalled Americans. Germany had invented a deadly, "invisible" weapon, the torpedo-firing submarine (or "U-boat"), and the German Navy followed a policy of unrestricted U-boat warfare against shipping destined for the British and French. *Any* shipping, not just enemy vessels, was fair game for the Germans. American warnings had persuaded them to give up this policy for a short time, but in early 1917 the Germans announced the resumption of unrestricted submarine warfare. On April 2, the President appeared before a joint session of Congress. Wilson asked for a declaration of war, and, four days later, Congress followed through.

The United States entered the war in opposition to Germany and Austria-Hungary (the Central Powers) and in alliance with Great Britain, France, Italy, and Japan (the Allies). Russia, which had entered the war on the side of the Allies, had been forced out of the war by the internal Bolshevik "October Revolution." President Wilson declared that the United States had no ambitions for territory or conquest; it only wanted "to make the world safe for democracy." Wilson outlined American war aims in his famous "Fourteen Points" speech in early 1918. He called for an end to imperialism and colonialism and urged that all nations of the world be given the right to control their own lives (what he called "self-determination"). He also advocated free trade and the establishment of an international peacekeeping organization, the League of Nations.

Despite Wilson's idealism, many Americans believed that the war against Germany, the principal enemy, was a war for civilization against the "Huns." Reprisals in the United States against people of German descent were commonplace. German culture was shunned. German music, including the works of Bach and Beethoven, vanished from the concert halls. U.S. culture was purged of German influence. Sauerkraut became "liberty cabbage."

American manpower and supplies turned the tide of the war in favor of the Allies. Both sides were exhausted by the time the United States entered the war. Although the American Expeditionary Force did not see combat until June 1918 and fought independent of Allied control, they soon made the difference. Germany could no longer fight, and it sued for peace. On November 11, 1918, a peace agreement, or *armistice*, was signed. The people of the world erupted in joyful celebration.

The final treaty of peace was to be negotiated at the French palace of Versailles in the spring of 1919. Wilson chose to lead the American peace delegation himself against the advice of his aides, who begged him not to risk his prestige. Wilson believed that he and he alone could get the Allies to adopt his Fourteen Points as the basis of the treaty. He refused to follow his aides' advice that he appoint a bipartisan peace delegation to ensure that the Republicans in the Senate would be willing to ratify the treaty. He sowed the seeds of the treaty's destruction with these decisions.

The President's triumphant arrival in Paris convinced him that the people of the world supported his goals. He was sadly mistaken. The leaders of Britain, France, and Italy were eager to dismantle Germany's empire and share the pieces among themselves. They were prepared to redraw the map of Europe to their own advantage; they did not encourage self-determination. They were willing to grant the U.S. President only the League of Nations, and the battered Wilson seized on this "concession" as the one redeeming feature of an otherwise harsh and vindictive treaty.

President Wilson sailed home, hoping that the extraordinary popularity he had enjoyed among the citizens of Europe had swayed American public opinion in favor of the treaty. But the Senate was not convinced. As Senators examined the treaty, many did not like what they read. Some focused on the President's failure to restrain the greed and anger of the European allies. Many disliked the proposed League of Nations, believing that it would damage American independence. Republican Henry Cabot Lodge of Massachusetts, the chairman of the Senate Foreign Relations Committee, proposed a set of "reservations" to the treaty focusing on the League.

Wilson reacted with stubborn anger. He insisted that the treaty was not simply the best he could get—it was a great treaty that the peoples of the world wanted and deserved. American refusal to ratify would destroy the world's hopes for an end to war. The war had been a war to end all wars. The Senate must not stand in the way of that great dream.

The President decided to go over the heads of the Senate to the American people. He campaigned across the nation, giving dozens of speeches in twenty-nine cities in three weeks from coast to coast urging adoption of the treaty. In Pueblo, Colorado, the President suffered a physical breakdown. He was rushed back to Washington, where he soon suffered a severe stroke. The President was crippled and bedridden, a virtual recluse in the White House. Mrs. Wilson took charge; some critics said that she was the acting President. Vice President Thomas R. Marshall was kept in the dark.

Despite his illness, Wilson refused to give in to pressures to accept the Lodge Reservations. But the Senate finally defeated the treaty. Wilson suggested to close friends that he should run for a third term, making the League of Nations the focus of the campaign, but he was persuaded to drop the idea; he could walk only haltingly, and with a cane. The Democratic nominee, Governor James M. Cox of Ohio, endorsed both the treaty and the League. His running-mate was Franklin D. Roosevelt, the young and handsome Assistant Secretary of the Navy. Many voters mistakenly thought that he was Theodore Roosevelt's son. Wilson watched from the sidelines, taking some comfort from having been awarded the 1920 Nobel Peace Prize.

The Republicans scented victory, but they were bitterly divided. In late 1918, they had been prepared to unite behind former President Roosevelt, but he had died suddenly in January 1919. Several candidates claimed to be Roosevelt's legitimate political heir. But the Republicans looked elsewhere. They found a "safe" candidate—an obscure Ohio Senator named Warren G. Harding. The handsome but vague former newspaper publisher had no obvious drawbacks, and he seemed tailor-made to capture the bloc of women voters enfranchised by the newly ratified Nineteenth Amendment. As his running-mate, the convention picked dour, silent Governor Calvin Coolidge of Massachusetts. The Vermont-born Coolidge had won national fame for his swift and brutal suppression of the Boston police strike of 1919.

Harding and Coolidge buried Cox and Roosevelt. Wilson despaired of the nation's judgment; he thought that his successor was an uncultured fool. But the nation was tired of war, tired of reform. The American people wanted to relax, and Harding and Coolidge promised "not nostrums, but normalcy."

CHAPTER SEVEN

THE REPUBLICAN REIGN

Warren Gamaliel Harding was in many ways a throwback to the days of McKinley. He had run a front-porch campaign, avoiding specifics about issues such as the Treaty of Versailles and the League of Nations. (A leading Republican boss, Boies Penrose, sent word to Harding's managers from his deathbed: "Keep Warren home. Don't let him make any speeches. If he does, someone's bound to ask questions, and Warren's just the sort of fool to try to answer them!") He planned to run a largely passive Presidency.

Harding's time in the Oval Office included a few notable achievements. The Washington Disarmament Conference of 1921, orchestrated by Secretary of State Charles Evans Hughes, resulted in an agreement by the United States, Britain, France, Italy, and Japan to limit the size of their navies. Harding made the first Presidential civil rights speech in the Deep South. He had several able advisers, among them Secretary of State Hughes and Secretary of Commerce Herbert Hoover.

But Harding's Administration was more famous for its scandals than its accomplishments. For every Hughes and

Hoover, Harding named two dunces, such as Secretary of the Navy Edwin Denby, and several outright crooks, such as Secretary of the Interior Albert B. Fall and Attorney General Harry Daugherty.

Harding knew his limits. He admitted that he was completely unqualified for the Presidency. He had suffered a nervous breakdown as a young man and had fragile nerves throughout his life. "My God!" he once exclaimed about the White House. "What is there in this job that a man should ever want to get into it?" His iron-willed wife was more ambitious than Harding. She had been the driving force behind his quest for the 1920 Republican Presidential nomination, and she enjoyed being First Lady far more then he enjoyed being President. Harding preferred to play poker with his cronies.

The Constitution had been amended in 1919 to prohibit the sale or manufacture of alcoholic beverages. *Prohibition,* the short term for the Eighteenth Amendment and the laws enacted to enforce it, was unpopular, but few politicians could afford to offend women's organizations, religious groups, and the Anti-Saloon League by opposing it. Still, the American people generally wanted a drink. The United States became a nation of law-breakers, from President Harding on down.

This free-and-easy attitude toward the law swept through the Harding Administration. The Attorney General could not be bothered to enforce the laws—he was too busy collecting payoffs for his refusal to crack down on bootleggers. The head of the Veterans' Bureau milked his agency dry at the expense of thousands of veterans.

The worst scandal involved Secretaries Fall and Denby and two tracts of land called oil reserves belonging to the Navy: Teapot Dome, Wyoming, and Elk Hills, Nevada. These oil fields were held in reserve in case of another war, when they would provide American warships with guaranteed fuel supplies. Secretary Fall persuaded the amiable Secretary Denby to transfer control of the oil reserves from the Navy Department to the Interior Department. Denby asked no questions. Fall made a killing for himself as oil company executives deluged him with bribes for permission to drill in the reserves. When necessary, Fall gave a tangled and dishonest explanation about how such drilling was actually for the benefit of maintaining the oil reserves. It sounded convincing if one did not look too closely.

The President was only dimly aware of the sleazy deals being struck all around him. He was personally honest in his public life. His private life was something else again. He tried to forget his cares by gambling and drinking with friends in a small Washington townhouse nicknamed "the little house on K Street." He had given up one long-time mistress, the handsome wife of a dry-goods merchant in his home town of Marion, Ohio, but he carried on an affair in a closet in the White House with a second mistress, a stenographer named Nan Britton, with whom he had a daughter.

Harding was sick, he was tired, and he was fed up. He had appointed former President Taft to be Chief Justice in 1921—and Taft repaid Harding's granting of his lifelong dream by bullying him to appoint conservative federal judges. Harding had named his friends to important jobs—and they had repaid him by stealing the country blind. As the President began to realize just how corrupt some of his appointees were, he became enraged. One visitor to the White House reported seeing Harding administering a terrible beating to Charles Forbes, the corrupt head of the Veterans' Bureau. Harding complained to the eminent journalist William Allen White, "I don't worry about my enemies—I can take care of them all right. It's my friends that keep me walking the floors at night!"

In the summer of 1923, the President made a cross-country Voyage of Understanding (in reality, a vacation) along the

Pacific Coast. He visited Alaska, the first President to do so, and several cities in the Northwest. During a rest stop in San Francisco, as he listened to his wife read a flattering magazine article about him, President Harding suddenly died.

Vice President Coolidge got the news of the President's death during a family visit at his father's home in Plymouth Notch, Vermont. The senior Coolidge, a justice of the peace and a notary public, administered the Presidential oath of office to his son by the light of a kerosene lamp. The scene dramatized Coolidge's appeal to the American people as a symbol of traditional American values.

By the end of 1923, the lid had blown off the scandals surrounding the Harding Administration. "Teapot Dome" became the catchphrase used to describe the whole sordid mess. Congressional and public investigations stunned the nation. A tight-lipped President Coolidge fired Attorney General Daugherty and appointed in his place the Dean of Columbia Law School, Harlan Fiske Stone. The two men had known each other since their student days at Amherst College, in Massachusetts, in the 1890s. Coolidge gave Stone a mandate—clean up the Administration—and Stone complied. The nation was reassured. The new President clearly had nothing to do with the mess in Washington.

Coolidge turned out to be the ultimate do-nothing President. He said little and slept twelve hours a day. He once woke from a long nap and asked, "Is the country still here?" He claimed that if you saw ten troubles heading for you, your best policy was to do nothing—nine would fall by the wayside, and you would have only one to deal with. He declared that "the business of America is business," and observed, "When more and more people are thrown out of work, unemployment tends to be the result." While Americans spent more and more and gambled recklessly on the stock market during the "Roaring Twenties," the President kept silent. Several economists, however, saw warning signs of a coming financial crash.

Coolidge won a term of his own in 1924 with the slogan "Keep Cool with Coolidge." He easily defeated the disorganized Democratic Party, whose convention had lasted for two weeks and 103 ballots before naming a Presidential candidate, a little-known corporation lawyer and former Solicitor General, John W. Davis. Disaffected liberals again split off from both parties and formed a new Progressive Party, led by Senator Robert LaFollette of Wisconsin.

Coolidge announced in 1928, "I do not choose to run." Some historians think that he was hinting that he wanted to be drafted for the nomination, but the Republicans took him at his word, naming Secretary of Commerce Herbert Hoover as their candidate. They counted on Hoover's worldwide fame and sterling record of efficiency, brilliance, and compassion. The man who had been the mastermind of American famine relief for Europe in 1918–1919 seemed unbeatable.

The Democrats chose Governor Alfred E. Smith of New York to oppose Hoover. Smith, the first Roman Catholic to be nominated for President by a major party, had close ties to voters from urban areas and the "newer" ethnic groups from Southern and Eastern Europe. He supported repeal of Prohibition. But his views and ties disturbed voters in the South and Midwest, and his religion brought out every hate group from under every rock across the land. They were more comfortable with the familiar and safe Hoover and elected him handily.

In the late 1920s, most Americans believed that the nation's economy was booming. Indeed, as President Hoover confidently predicted in his inaugural address in March 1929, poverty might well vanish from American life once and for all. But some economists were deeply worried. They argued that the ever-rising stock market was overdue for a major tumble. A crash would bury millions of Americans who had plunged into the gamble of buying and trading stock.

The crash finally came in October 1929. On October 24

and again on October 29, the bottom fell out of the New York Stock Exchange. Within two weeks, stock prices plunged so far that $30 billion in the market value of listed stocks vanished. By mid-1932, this figure had more than doubled, to $75 billion. The Great Crash was the opening act of the severest economic catastrophe in American history.

The effects of the Crash, which eventually developed into what historians call the Great Depression, did not show themselves overnight. But as month succeeded month and the ripples from the Crash spread throughout the economy, all agreed that the economic "miracle" of the 1920s was finally over. Factories shut their gates and closed, and millions of frightened citizens lost their jobs. Had that "miracle" ever been real? The businessman had been the hero of the 1920s, but Americans no longer admired the businessman in the 1930s. Instead, they demanded a solution to the crisis.

President Hoover recognized the seriousness of the situation, but he believed that the free-enterprise system, like a huge and complex self-regulating machine, would fix itself. Prosperity, he kept saying, was "just around the corner." The President's promise grew ever more hollow as the promised turnaround failed to materialize.

Most Americans had never looked to government for aid in dealing with problems such as debt and unemployment and the difficulty of finding an income in old age. Most people were on their own and accepted this as the way of the world. But the consequences of the Depression seemed much too monumental a problem for too many people to rely on self-help and private charity. Financially strapped state and city governments did what they could, but they were far from certain that they could assume the burden of relief programs. The American people remembered Hoover's accomplishments in providing food, medicine, and other supplies to war-torn Europe in the years after the First World War. Surely Hoover would meet this challenge at home as well.

The problem was that the President believed that the federal government should not give direct relief to the unemployed. He argued that a national relief policy would violate the Constitution's limits on the powers of the federal government. He held these views in good faith, and he had some basis for them. But as the Depression worsened, many Americans decided that the President did not care about their plight. They made fun of Hoover, but their jokes were filled with anger and despair. A torn jacket stuffed with newspapers was called a "Hoover overcoat." A broken-down car pulled by horses was a "Hoovermobile." Most famous of all, the communities of tar-paper and balsa-wood shacks built by homeless Americans in cities across the nation were "Hoovervilles."

One incident ruined Hoover's reputation. At the end of the First World War, Congress had agreed to establish a program to pay American veterans a cash bonus. In 1931, Congress passed a law over Hoover's veto allowing veterans to get from the government loans of 50 percent of the value of their bonus. The next year, Democratic leaders in Congress suggested that the whole bonus be paid in cash. Veterans' groups marched on Washington to press for laws authorizing the payment of the whole cash bonus. The "Bonus Army" marchers brought their wives and children to show the President and Congress their collective plight. Many had no homes. The President refused to hear their pleas. The seventeen thousand marchers camped in Washington, declaring that they would not leave the city unless the bonus bill succeeded. When the bill failed in the Senate, the government offered to pay the veterans' travel costs home, but two thousand stayed put. They had no place else to go. District of Columbia police clashed with the homeless veterans; two police officers and two veterans died in the fighting. The President then called out federal soldiers under the command of General Douglas MacArthur and his aide, Major Dwight D. Eisenhower, to disperse the "Bonus Army." The soldiers used tear gas, tanks, and flamethrowers to demolish the "Hooverville." Soldiers wearing gas masks and carrying rifles with fixed bayonets arrested the fleeing veterans and their families. Motion-picture newsreels showing the violence stunned the nation.

The 1932 Republican convention grimly renominated President Hoover. There was no alternative candidate. In November, the unpopular President was turned out of office. Many voters were doubtless swayed by the Democrats' promise to repeal the Eighteenth Amendment. But the real issue was the Depression. Thirteen million Americans were without employment; thousands of families were still living in makeshift shacks; farmers were rioting; hunger was rampant; and most of the nation's banks were closed or about to close. The victorious candidate, Democratic Governor Franklin D. Roosevelt of New York, seemed confident and able. No one was sure what he would do, or could do, about the Depression—but the American people were willing to give him a chance.

CHAPTER EIGHT
FRANKLIN D. ROOSEVELT

Franklin Delano Roosevelt has set the model for all his successors, and generations of American voters have measured candidates for the Presidency by Roosevelt's standard. As with Abraham Lincoln, Roosevelt used the powers of the Presidency to lead the nation in dealing with a grave crisis.

Roosevelt was the only child of wealthy landowners in upstate New York. He was educated in private schools and at Harvard College and Columbia Law School. In 1905, he married his fifth cousin once removed, Eleanor Roosevelt, the niece of President Theodore Roosevelt, who gave the bride away at the wedding. He joined President Woodrow Wilson's Administration as Assistant Secretary of the Navy, the same post from which Theodore Roosevelt had begun his national political career. Unlike most other members of the family, Franklin Roosevelt was a Democrat. The handsome, charming New Yorker loyally accepted the Vice Presidential nomination on the doomed 1920 Democratic ticket, knowing that loyalty in politics is rewarded sooner or later. He seemed to have a great future.

Roosevelt's hopes disintegrated in 1921. While on a family

vacation in Campobello, in New Brunswick, Canada, Roosevelt caught a chill after swimming in the Bay of Fundy that led to polio, or infantile paralysis, a dreaded disease until the 1950s. Roosevelt lost the use of his legs for the rest of his life. His heartbroken mother told him that he should retire to the family estate at Hyde Park, New York, along the Hudson River, and give up all thought of a career in politics.

But the illness transformed Roosevelt. From an amiable but superficial aristocrat with an intellectual bent toward social justice, he became a fully committed reformer who *felt* people's suffering and burned to remedy it. He grew to share his wife's compassion and interest in reform. She became her husband's partner and tutor as he taught himself about the problems facing the United States.

Roosevelt's revived political career grew out of this newfound, deep passion for social justice. By 1932, he was the popular and respected Governor of New York, a central figure in national Democratic politics, and the leading candidate for his party's Presidential nomination. He triumphed at the convention in Chicago, Illinois, after a sharp and bitter contest with his rival and former friend Al Smith. Breaking tradition, Roosevelt flew to Chicago to accept the nomination in person. He wanted to prove he could get around, and he knew his appearance would electrify the convention and the nation. He was right. His promise of "a new deal for the American people" was enthusiastically received. In a whirlwind campaign, FDR spoke to audiences large and small, jousted and joked with reporters, and projected precisely the image of confidence that Hoover had called for and yet seemed so far from achieving. The Democrats overwhelmed Hoover, scoring their first lopsided victory in generations.

In February 1933, the month before his inauguration, Roosevelt narrowly escaped being murdered in Miami after a fishing vacation. As FDR sat immobilized, with ten pounds of steel braces around his legs, in an open touring car with

Mayor Anton Cermak of Chicago, a bitter thirty-two-year-old brick mason named Giuseppe Zangara, who had been in constant torment from a stomach operation, shouted, "Too many people are starving to death." He fired his cheap gun five times at the car from a park bench thirty-five feet away. The President-elect was unscathed, but Mayor Cermak was wounded, and he died two weeks later. As Roosevelt cradled the wounded man in his arms, Cermak whispered, "I'm glad it was me instead of you." The killer was electrocuted in mid-March, two weeks after Roosevelt's inauguration.

March 4, Inauguration Day, dawned cloudy and cheerless. The glum and downcast Hoover and the somber Roosevelt rode side by side in the Presidential limousine to the Capitol's East Front, where 100,000 anxious witnesses were waiting. The retiring President was bitter toward his successor, who had refused Hoover's plea to work together in the days leading up to the transfer of power. The thirty-second President had his own ideas, and he wanted to make a clean break with the past. His Inaugural Address, delivered in a cold wind, did not mince words. Holding tight to the rostrum, he declared what everyone knew to be the case: The American economy had all but ground to a halt, and drastic action was needed. He promised "action, and action now." He described the Depression as a crisis as serious as any war the nation had faced, a "dark hour of our national life." Crisis measures were necessary.

Roosevelt's pledge of action lifted the spirits of the American people and gave meaning to his ringing declaration, "The only thing we have to fear is fear itself—nameless, unreasoning, unjustified terror which paralyzes needed efforts to convert retreat into advance." Happiness, he said, "lies not in the mere possession of money; it lies in the joy of achievement, in the thrill of creative effort." The family Bible on which Franklin Roosevelt took the oath of office from Chief Justice Hughes lay open to 1 Corinthians: "And now abideth faith, hope, charity, these three; but the greatest of these is charity."

The next three months—known as "the Hundred Days"—were a whirlwind of Presidential proclamations, bills, and executive orders. Roosevelt delivered the first of his famous radio broadcasts, the "fireside chats." The President took the American people into his confidence, explaining each new measure step by step so that the people felt that they understood and had a part in the new effort to fight the Depression. Congress cooperated with joy and relief, often passing bills the members had not even read.

Roosevelt knew how dangerous the situation was. Most people had all but despaired of any solution to the Depression that was consistent with the Constitution. Some called openly for a dictatorship, whether of the Left or the Right. The President's great object—and great achievement—was to convince the people that the government could cope with the country's problems without having to destroy government of, by, and for the people.

The Roosevelt Administration's program, dubbed the New Deal, swept out of the capital and through the nation like a tornado. It had two goals: (1) to get direct aid to the victims of the Depression and (2) to get the economy back on its feet. Hundreds of bright young men and women, graduates of the nation's leading universities, overran Washington to run the New Deal programs. Reporters nicknamed them "Felix's happy hot dogs," after their mentor, Professor Felix Frankfurter of the Harvard Law School. They staffed a bewildering collection of agencies—NRA, WPA, PWA, HOLC, AAA, CCC, and so forth. These were the "alphabet agencies," and the people running them and advising the President were called the "brains trust."

The centerpiece of the first wave of New Deal programs was the National Recovery Administration (NRA), whose symbol was the "blue eagle." The idea behind the NRA was that cut-

FRANKLIN D. ROOSEVELT — 87

Franklin Delano Roosevelt, the thirty-second President (1933–1945), has been the only Chief Executive to win more than two terms. He died of a cerebral hemorrhage three months after his fourth inauguration (the only one ever held in the White House). His "New Deal" guided the nation through the Great Depression. FDR, as he was popularly dubbed by tabloid newspapers, was our greatest "war President," directing the Allied powers to victory over Germany, Japan, and Italy in the Second World War. He was also the first "media President," making effective use of "fireside chats" over the radio to the American people and witty, jovial, off-the-cuff press conferences in the Oval Office.

throat competition among businesses had helped to drop prices and wages, making the Depression worse. If you regulated competition, the economy would recover its strength. The NRA organized industries into groups that would write codes, or sets of rules, governing prices and quality of goods and wages. Any company violating its industry's code could be prosecuted under federal law.

The NRA was not successful—and within two years the Supreme Court killed it. In the famous "sick chicken" case, *Schechter Poultry Corp. v. United States*, the Justices unanimously agreed that the NRA was unconstitutional because Congress had handed over its lawmaking powers to an executive agency, which in turn had handed these powers to private companies.

Secretly, the President was relieved that the Court had killed the NRA. The Justices had disposed of a failed program, saving the President the embarrassing task of shutting down the NRA himself. But the Justices sharpened their axes and went after other New Deal programs. They claimed that the programs violated private property rights protected by the Constitution and that Congress had gone too far in trying to use its power to regulate interstate commerce. The Court struck down New Deal measures designed to relieve the plight of the poor and powerless—farmers, mine workers, those who could not pay off mortgages on their homes. The small liberal group on the Court—Justices Louis D. Brandeis, Harlan Fiske Stone, and Benjamin Nathan Cardozo, occasionally joined by Chief Justice Charles Evans Hughes—protested bitterly against these decisions, but to no avail.

Roosevelt and the nation were outraged. To be sure, some of the New Deal laws were badly drafted and should have been struck down. But it seemed that the Supreme Court was standing in the way of the government's efforts to solve the problems of the Depression.

Roosevelt made the election of 1936 a referendum on his policies, and the voters rallied to his call. He carried every one of the forty-eight states except Maine and Vermont. (He was sworn in on January 20, 1937—the first President to take office under the Twentieth Amendment, which pushed back the start of the Presidential and Congressional terms from March to January to eliminate "lame duck" sessions of Congress.) The people liked the New Deal. They liked that the government had put millions of jobless Americans to work building bridges, post offices, schools, roads, libraries, and dams. They liked the new Social Security program, which gave retired and disabled Americans a source of income. They were convinced that the government now cared about and understood their problems and was willing to help.

Roosevelt decided that the people had given him a mandate to move against the Supreme Court. He made a speech in which he argued that the "Nine Old Men" were tired and overworked and needed help. He suggested that Congress adopt a law allowing the President to name a new Justice for every sitting Justice over seventy years of age who did not retire from the Court, up to a maximum of six. If enacted, the Court reorganization plan would have given the President a guaranteed majority on the Court to support his programs against the conservative Justices.

Many Americans were shaken by Roosevelt's idea, which quickly became known as the "Court-packing" plan. They believed that the proposal, if adopted, would destroy the independence of the Court and as a result might destroy the Constitution. Many members of Roosevelt's own party opposed the bill. The Justices countered with a shrewd move of their own. Chief Justice Hughes and Justice Brandeis joined with conservative Justice Willis Van Devanter to draft a response by the Chief Justice to a question from Senator Burton K. Wheeler of Montana, an opponent of the plan. Hughes explained that the Court was easily keeping up with its work and that the Roosevelt plan would actually hamper the Justices' efforts to handle their workload. At the same time, the Court announced a major decision. It upheld the National Labor Relations Act, a law that labor unions revered as "labor's Bill of Rights." The decision signaled that the Justices would not stand in the way of all New Deal measures. And then Justice Van Devanter finally resigned, giving the

President his first chance to appoint a Justice to the Supreme Court. These steps, and the sudden death of the Senate Majority Leader, the floor leader for the Court reorganization bill, killed the measure. It was a significant defeat for the President.

Roosevelt's second term was also complicated by foreign policy issues. He watched helplessly as the Nazi dictatorship in Germany and the Fascist dictatorship in Italy expanded their power by subversion and conquest. He also worried about Japan's efforts to carve out a Pacific empire. The American people, however, did not share Roosevelt's concerns. They had bitter memories of the "war to end all wars," the Treaty of Versailles, and the toothless League of Nations, and they wanted to stay out of foreign wars. They did feel some concern about Japan's expansionism, but they did not take the Japanese seriously as a military power.

Roosevelt urged in several of his speeches that the free powers of the world "quarantine the aggressors" through an economic boycott—an idea that other nations did not adopt. He denounced German takeovers of Austria and Czechoslovakia and the Italian conquest of Ethiopia. And his Administration applied constant pressure to the Japanese, demanding that Japan limit its expansion into China and the Pacific islands.

In September 1939, war broke out in Europe. The line-up startled Americans, for the Soviet Union allied itself with Germany, Italy, and Japan. Germany and the U.S.S.R. carved up Poland in a few weeks, but most Americans did not care. The "America First" movement argued that the war was not America's problem and that Europe was doomed anyway. If the United States entered the war to support Britain and France, they predicted, the United States would be doomed as well.

Other Americans believed that the United States had to aid Britain and France in order to protect American interests and the cause of freedom. Many American volunteers joined British and Canadian military units. When France fell in the spring of 1940 and Winston S. Churchill became Britain's new Prime Minister, Americans were stirred by his eloquence and courage. Journalists such as Edward R. Murrow of CBS reported on the heroism of the people of London, who were enduring daily bombing raids by the German Air Force.

The 1940 Presidential campaign was not politics as usual. President Roosevelt had surveyed the field of candidates vying to succeed him and believed that none of them was up to the job. Therefore, he decided that he would have to break tradition and run for an unprecedented third term. Republicans—and some Democrats—were infuriated that he was challenging a tradition that George Washington had begun nearly 150 years earlier. Campaign buttons read: "WASHINGTON WOULDN'T. GRANT COULDN'T. ROOSEVELT SHOULDN'T." In reply, the Democrats argued that it would be foolish to "change horses in the middle of a stream." The Republican candidate, Wendell Willkie, charged that the President would drag the nation into war in Europe. Roosevelt angrily replied, "Your boys are *not* going to go off to die in foreign wars." The President did win his third term but by a narrower margin than he had amassed in 1932 or in 1936.

In 1941, President Roosevelt took two major steps closer to taking sides with the Allies. He proposed that the United States "be the great arsenal of democracy" and put forward a remarkable program called Lend-Lease. The British would receive fifty old but usable American destroyers in exchange for ninety-nine-year leases on British bases in the Western Hemisphere. Roosevelt explained his reasoning by analogy: A neighbor's house is on fire, and he asks to borrow your garden hose. All you want to do is to lend him the hose to put out the fire and get it back when the fire is out. That summer, FDR held a secret meeting with Prime Minister Churchill. In

August, American and British ships rendezvoused in Canadian waters, and the two leaders conferred amiably for two days. In a joint statement, the Atlantic Charter, they called for "final destruction of the Nazi tyranny" and affirmed their hopes for peace, freedom for the world's peoples, and a strong new international peace-keeping structure. These and other initiatives indicated that Roosevelt saw American involvement in the war as inevitable, but he did not commit the nation to war.

When America did enter the war four months later, it was not a foreign war any longer. On December 7, 1941, the Japanese Navy and Air Force staged a surprise raid on Pearl Harbor, Hawaii, the site of the largest U.S. Pacific naval base. The Japanese destroyed 19 ships, including 8 battleships, and 188 aircraft and killed 2,280 military personnel and 68 civilians. The Pearl Harbor attack was only one element of an array of Japanese strategic raids throughout the Pacific. At the time, Japanese diplomats were still in "friendly" negotiations with American Secretary of State Cordell Hull in Washington, D.C. Most historians agree that the Administration expected some sort of large-scale Japanese move somewhere in the Pacific but that Roosevelt and his aides were stunned that the Japanese would actually strike at American territory.

The next day, President Roosevelt appeared before a joint session of Congress. His speech took just six minutes. In clear, angry prose that he had written himself, the President ticked off the numerous attacks the Japanese had launched, declaring December 7 to be "a date which will live in infamy." Congress immediately voted to declare that a state of war existed between the United States and Japan—a formula designed to conform to a 1928 treaty under which all the nations of the world, including the United States and Japan, had renounced war as an instrument of foreign policy. A couple of days later, Germany's *Führer*, Adolf Hitler, who had not wanted the United States drawn into any war, declared war on the United States, and Italy's *Duce*, Benito Mussolini, followed suit. (In the summer of 1941, the U.S.S.R. had switched sides, because Hitler had turned on his former ally.) Congress quickly replied in kind. The war was truly a world war now.

The course of the conflict aged Roosevelt terribly. Photographs taken in 1932, when FDR was fifty, show a calm, strong, jaunty President. By 1945, he looked at least ten years older than his sixty-three years. The demands of war abroad and coordinating the war effort at home were such that he felt that he could not abandon the helm or delegate the burdens of office. Again, as with the need to frame the government's response to the economic crisis of the Depression, the Second World War concentrated vast authority in the hands of the President of the United States. But that authority was a crushing weight for even the strongest and most confident President to bear.

As the war progressed, Roosevelt set in motion two projects that were destined to shape the postwar world. The first, and more hopeful, was his dream of an international peacekeeping agency that would have the teeth that the League of Nations had lacked: the United Nations. The second, which the President approved almost casually, resulted from suggestions from leading scientists, including Albert Einstein. Einstein informed the President that major advances in nuclear physics suggested that the atom could be split—an achievement that would be a source of great energy, perhaps of a weapon using that source of energy. The President approved a secret project, code-named the Manhattan Project, to carry out research and development work on an atomic weapon. At bases in Los Alamos, New Mexico, and Oak Ridge, Tennessee, the scientists and technicians of the Manhattan Project designed and built a new weapon—the atomic bomb.

Like President Lincoln during the Civil War, President

Roosevelt believed that the ordinary processes of government should carry on during wartime. Thus, the United States held a Presidential election campaign in 1944. Roosevelt ran for a fourth term against the young, vigorous Republican nominee, Governor Thomas E. Dewey of New York. The diminutive, mustached Dewey looked to many Americans like "the man on the wedding cake," and he seemed too inexperienced to lead the United States in wartime. Roosevelt won a fourth term despite his weariness—and his failing health. He did not know that he was a dying man; his doctors were deeply concerned about the state of his health, but they could not bring themselves to tell the President that a fourth term might kill him.

Like most other Presidents, Roosevelt did not pay much attention to the selection of his Vice Presidential running mates. His first, John Nance Garner of Texas, the former Speaker of the House, described the office as "not worth a bucket of warm spit." Garner retired in 1940—no one has been Vice President for more than two terms—and was succeeded by Secretary of Agriculture Henry A. Wallace. As the 1944 election approached, leaders of the Democratic Party began to worry about Wallace's erratic views and gushing admiration for the newest major nation to join the Allies, the Soviet Union. Roosevelt was persuaded to dump Wallace and to run with Senator Harry S Truman of Missouri, an able legislator whose investigations of government waste in the war effort had saved the United States tens of millions of dollars. Neither man realized how fateful this change would be.

Roosevelt began his fourth term with a brief inaugural ceremony at the White House, the only time since the capital moved to Washington that the Inauguration has not taken place at the Capitol. He then flew off to a meeting with Churchill and Soviet leader Joseph Stalin at Yalta, a resort on the Black Sea in the U.S.S.R. For whatever reason, he never fully briefed Vice President Truman about the war effort or the Manhattan Project. In early April, the exhausted President decided that he needed a rest. He traveled to Warm Springs, Georgia, a favorite vacation spot because he believed that its waters helped restore some feeling and movement in his wasted legs. On April 12, 1945, while his portrait was being painted, he complained of "a terrific headache." Suddenly he slumped forward, unconscious. He died later that day of a massive cerebral hemorrhage, an especially serious kind of stroke.

Roosevelt's death was the end of an era. Many Americans could not remember a time when he had not been President. The nation went into deep mourning, as did the people of Great Britain, France, and the other Allies. The new President, Harry S Truman, expressed the feelings of his countrymen when he said that it was "as if the sun, the moon, and all the planets had fallen in on me." For more than four decades, the United States has lived and governed itself in the shadow of FDR.

CHAPTER NINE

"GIVE 'EM HELL, HARRY" AND "I LIKE IKE"

Harry S Truman was the last man to be President who had not gone to college. He was a self-taught student of history, a pretty good piano player, a failed businessman, and a veteran of the First World War, Missouri politics, and the U.S. Senate. Most Americans could not help comparing him unfavorably with Franklin D. Roosevelt, the only President many of them had known. But Truman had a solid core of intelligence, shrewdness, and common sense that shaped his Presidency.

When Truman became President, he faced an unprecedented decision: whether to use the atomic bomb. Truman had only the faintest idea of what the Manhattan Project was. When, as chairman of a Senate committee looking into waste in government war spending, he had tried to investigate the Manhattan Project, he had been warned off with no explanation. As Vice President, Truman was still in the dark about the effort to develop an atomic weapon. President Truman was stunned when Secretary of War Henry Stimson and the directors of the Manhattan Project briefed him about the bomb. Three months later, on July 20, 1945, the first atomic bomb was tested successfully at Trinity Site, Alamogordo, in the New Mexico desert.

At the beginning of the Manhattan Project, everyone had assumed that the bomb would be used against Nazi Germany. But the Germans had surrendered unconditionally on May 7, 1945—known as V-E Day. The Japanese were still fighting, however. Allied forces were posed for an all-out amphibious assault on the Japanese homeland, but worried generals advised the President that the attack would result in millions of casualties on both sides. Perhaps, President Truman reasoned, dropping the atomic bomb would actually cause fewer deaths and injuries than an all-out invasion.

Truman decided that he would order the use of the first bomb on a Japanese city. The devastation it would cause would put irresistible pressure on the Japanese to surrender. The President rejected some scientists' pleas to drop the bomb on an uninhabited island or desert. He believed that such a test would not give convincing proof to the Japanese of its power.

An American B-29 bomber, the *Enola Gay*, dropped "Little Boy" on the industrial city of Hiroshima on August 6, 1945. But the Japanese did not immediately surrender because they could not believe their own reports of what had happened. The President ordered the dropping of another atomic bomb. A second B-29, *Bock's Car*, dropped "Fat Man" on Nagasaki. President Truman worried as to what he would have to do if the second bomb did not persuade the Japanese to surrender. The United States had had only two bombs in its arsenal after the July test and now had used both. The only choice remaining was a full-scale invasion. But the second bomb did its work. Emperor Hirohito overruled his generals and advisers and agreed to surrender unconditionally.

The war's end brought new problems. Truman felt an obligation to make President Roosevelt's dream of the United Nations a reality. In addition, the victorious Allies had to decide what to do about war-ravaged Europe and the old colonial empires.

The major foreign-policy issue facing the President was the Soviet Union. Americans distrusted the U.S.S.R. and the U.S.S.R. feared and distrusted the West. This mutual suspicion was based partly on different ideologies and economic systems. Many Americans feared that the Communist Party in the United States was nothing more than an arm of the Soviet Union. For their part, Stalin and his successors shared the ages-old Russian distrust of the outside world and its motives.

And so a "Cold War" of spies and subversion followed the Second World War. Soviet agents had infiltrated the Manhattan Project and learned top-secret military data that gave Moscow the missing links it needed to solve the problem of making atomic weapons. (Congressional critics of the Truman Administration charged that the Soviet Union never would have developed the atomic bomb without the aid of traitors in the United States. This was not true; all the "atom spies" had done was to shave a few years off the Soviet atomic program's timetable.)

President Truman was sensitive to charges, principally Republican, that there were nests of Soviet spies and saboteurs in the government. He took vigorous anti-Communist measures, though some violated individual liberties protected by the Constitution. To monitor Soviet activities and combat Soviet espionage, he founded the National Security Council (NSC) and the Central Intelligence Agency (CIA). In his retirement, Truman declared that creating the CIA was his worst mistake as President.

President Truman proposed domestic programs as bold and inventive as anything in the New Deal. He pursued a vigorous policy of civil rights. He was the first President to appoint a Civil Rights Commission. Its tough-minded report showed the nation just how broad and how deep the stain of racism and prejudice had spread. The commission's findings scandalized the nation—and angered Southern Democrats. Truman sponsored the creation of a Fair Employment Practices Commission (FEPC). He urged the adoption of a government program to assist ordinary people in paying major medical bills. He brought former President Herbert Hoover out of retirement to lead a special commission on the reorganization of the Presidency and the executive branch of government. The Hoover Commission's report helped to bring the executive branch in line with the requirements of the postwar world.

In 1948, the Democrats were badly split. President Truman's Administration was plagued with scandal. Several of his aides had been forced to resign. Former Vice President Henry Wallace, denouncing Truman for starting the Cold War and for his hostility to the Soviets, founded a new Progressive Party and became its candidate for President. On the right wing of the party, Governor J. Strom Thurmond of South Carolina led his fellow Southerners out of the Democratic Convention when liberals led by Mayor Hubert H. Humphrey of Minneapolis, Minnesota, won the floor battle to endorse black Americans' demands for equality and justice. Thurmond and other Southern Democrats formed the "Dixiecrat" Party. What was left of the Democratic Party closed ranks behind President Truman. Some party leaders hoped that he would step aside so that they could nominate General Dwight D. Eisenhower, the Supreme Allied Commander in Europe in the Second World War. Eisenhower dashed their hopes when he disclosed that he was a Republican.

The Republican Presidential nominee, Governor Thomas E. Dewey of New York, seemed to have a lock on the election. Dewey had lost to Franklin D. Roosevelt in 1944. This time, he was so confident of his coming victory that he began to act as if he were already President.

Harry Truman was the only major political figure who was

convinced that the election was not over until the last ballot had been counted. He campaigned across the nation by train. During his "whistle-stop" tour, he denounced the "do-nothing" Republican-dominated Congress for blocking his programs. His supporters dubbed Truman's struggle the "Give 'em Hell" campaign. Truman replied, "I'm not giving them hell. I'm telling the truth, and they think it's hell." The *Chicago Tribune* proclaimed on the night of Election Day 1948: "DEWEY DEFEATS TRUMAN." Truman and the Democrats had the last laugh: Truman won re-election, beating Dewey and the others narrowly in the popular vote and decisively in the Electoral College. And the Democrats took back control of both houses of Congress, which they had lost in the 1946 midterm election.

The full term of office that Truman won in 1948 was even more eventful than the preceding forty-five and a half months had been. Nothing seemed certain—not even the White House. The President discovered structural problems in the White House that threatened to cause its collapse, and ordered that it be thoroughly reconstructed. He and his family took up temporary residence in Blair House, across the street. A band of terrorists seeking independence for Puerto Rico attacked Blair House but failed to get off even one shot at the President.

On the world front, the Truman Administration stood by helplessly as Mao Zedong and Zhou Enlai led Communist forces to final victory in China in October 1949, compelling the anti-Communist Nationalists, led by Chiang Kai-shek, to flee to the island of Taiwan. Republicans gleefully charged that Truman had "lost" China to the Communists. (Truman declined the opportunity to discuss personally with Mao and Zhou, in Washington, D.C., the future of U.S.–China relations.)

Most important of all, the President led the United States into a new armed conflict in 1950. As a result of the Second

World War, the Asian nation of Korea, once occupied by the Japanese, had been partitioned. North Korea was a Communist state under the domination of China and the Soviet Union, and South Korea was friendly to the West. In June 1950, the North Korean army crossed the boundary between the two nations and invaded the South. The Korean Conflict had begun.

For three years, the United States and other members of the United Nations fought a "police action" against North Korea and, ultimately, China. In 1951, President Truman locked horns with General Douglas MacArthur, the supreme American commander in Korea and the officer who had led the Army in breaking up the "Bonus Army" in 1932. MacArthur had thrown back a major Chinese attack on South Korea and then advanced far into North Korea. He wanted to cross the Yalu River and take "the preponderance of Allied power" into China. President Truman repeatedly ordered against such measures, but General MacArthur was unwilling to obey. President Truman invoked his constitutional authority as Commander-in-Chief and fired MacArthur for "rank insubordination" a few months after flying 14,500 miles to Wake Island in the Pacific to try to reach an understanding face to face. The American people reacted with anger at first, demonstrating support for the hero of the Second World War. But the President stood his ground, and in time the people came to agree with him. Truman vindicated the central principle of civilian supremacy over the military.

A problem related to the Korean Conflict led to a confrontation over the limits on Presidential power. A crippling steel strike threatened the war effort. The President issued an executive order seizing the steel mills and drafting the striking workers into the Army. The President claimed that he had inherent authority under the Constitution to protect the national security by such means. But the Supreme Court ruled that Truman had overstepped his powers. He was angered by the Court's decision but obeyed it. The strike was settled by ordinary means.

In 1952, President Truman thought about running again for a second full term of his own. In 1946, the Republican-controlled Congress had struck at the late President Roosevelt. It had proposed, and the states had ratified, the Twenty-Second Amendment, which bars any future President from more than two terms in office. President Truman was exempt from the two-term limit but decided not to run—in part because he believed that he might not win. In addition to dissatisfaction over the Korean Conflict, several scandals involving members of Truman's staff tainted the reputation of his Administration. Republicans tauntingly asked, "Had enough?"

The 1952 election became a referendum on Korea and the "Truman scandals." The Democrats nominated the eloquent liberal Governor of Illinois, Adlai E. Stevenson. (Stevenson's grandfather had been Grover Cleveland's second Vice President.) The Republicans chose former General Dwight D. Eisenhower to bear their standard; Senator Richard M. Nixon of California was his running-mate.

Eisenhower was the first Presidential candidate to make use of modern advertising methods in his campaign. His advertising agency coined the slogan "I Like Ike." The General campaigned as a peace candidate. He declared, "I will go to Korea" to end the long war there. He also ran as a vigorous anti-Communist. Documented charges about scandals involving Senator Nixon had no effect on Eisenhower's popularity. The Republicans swamped the Democrats and moved into the White House for the first time in twenty years.

Eisenhower served two full terms as President, contending with anti-Communist hysteria at home and the Cold War abroad. He depended heavily on his chief of staff, the cold and efficient Sherman Adams, a former Governor of New Hampshire, for the day-to-day running of his Administration, and on his combative Secretary of State, John Foster Dulles, for the conduct of foreign policy, which sometimes ran to *brinkmanship*, that is, taking disputes with the U.S.S.R. to the edge of war. His Cabinet was nicknamed "eight millionaires and a plumber [the Secretary of Labor]."

President Eisenhower had to contend with anti-Communist witch-hunts conducted by the House Un-American Activities Committee and by Senator Joseph R. McCarthy of Wisconsin. He reluctantly oversaw the federal government's enforcement of civil rights legislation and the momentous federal court decisions ordering desegregation of the nation's schools. In 1958, to enforce a Supreme Court decision resisted by the Governor of Arkansas and the state's National Guard, Eisenhower put the state's National Guard under his own command and sent the 101st Airborne Division to enforce the law of the land. During his Administration, the interstate highway system and the American space program were born. The Korean Conflict ended in an uncomfortable stalemate for both sides.

Eisenhower was one of the oldest Presidents in our history. He suffered several serious bouts of ill health, including a heart attack, that caused many Americans to worry about the problems of Presidential disability and succession. He managed to recover from these illnesses and arranged with Vice President Nixon the first detailed measures for coping with Presidential illnesses. Eisenhower was the first President to be bound by the two-term limit of the Twenty-Second Amendment.

In his 1961 annual message to Congress, President Eisenhower performed one last public service to the nation, warning of the growing power in American life of the "military-industrial complex"—that is, the network of defense contractors and government agencies that wielded ever-increasing power over American diplomatic, budget, and defense policies. The nation has been slow to heed his warning.

CHAPTER TEN

"THE CHALLENGING, REVOLUTIONARY SIXTIES": KENNEDY, LYNDON JOHNSON, NIXON

The 1960 Presidential campaign featured two Presidential candidates born in the twentieth century. Senator John F. Kennedy, a Massachusetts Democrat and the first Catholic Presidential candidate since Al Smith in 1928, declared himself to be in the tradition of Jefferson, Wilson, Franklin D. Roosevelt, and Truman. (Truman supported fellow Missourian Stuart Symington for the White House, and Eleanor Roosevelt preferred Adlai Stevenson.) He sparred with Vice President Nixon, the Republican nominee, in four television "debates." In one of the closest elections in the history of the Presidency, Kennedy narrowly defeated Nixon and became, at forty-three, the youngest man ever elected to the Presidency.

John Kennedy's inaugural address was an eloquent call to battle, to service, and to achievement: "Ask not, my fellow Americans, what your country can do for you—ask what you can do for your country." He and his wife, Jacqueline, set standards of style, elegance, and culture. He inspired the young people of America to consider careers in government and public service through the creation of such organizations as the Peace Corps and the Alliance for Progress. He held frequent televised press conferences. His enthusiastic support for the American space program helped the United States to recover lost ground in the "space race" with the Soviet Union. He challenged the nation to achieve his goal of landing a man on the Moon and returning him safely to Earth before the end of the decade.

His Administration had problems as well. In 1961, a secret operation that had been planned by the Eisenhower Administration against the new Communist leader of Cuba, Fidel Castro, led to the botched Bay of Pigs invasion. A force of 1,500 anti-Castro Cubans was overwhelmed on the beaches; thousands were killed or captured by Castro's army. Castro was a nagging worry for the President. Kennedy authorized several secret, illegal operations, some with Mafia aid, designed either to assassinate Castro or otherwise to discredit him and remove him from office.

There was no actual "shooting war" in Europe, but the continent became a chessboard in the Cold War. A summit meeting in Vienna, Austria, in the spring of 1961 with Soviet leader Nikita Khrushchev left Kennedy bruised and shaken. In the summer of 1962, a crisis developed in the divided nation of Germany. East Germany was ruled by a Communist government supported by Soviet army units; West Germany was allied with the anti-Communist nations of Western Europe and the United States. Berlin, the former German capital, was deep in the heart of East Germany but itself was divided into Communist and anti-Communist zones. That summer, the Soviet Union built a wall that cut Berlin in two. The Berlin Wall still stands today as a symbol of the Cold War.

During Kennedy's three years in office, Southeast Asia became the principal focus of East-West tensions. Communist forces controlling North Vietnam worked with guerrillas in South Vietnam and Laos to overthrow neutralist or anti-

Communist regimes in those countries. The President supported these regimes with American aid and advisers. At the beginning of November 1963, Kennedy and his aides agreed that the President of South Vietnam, Ngo Dinh Diem, could no longer be relied on, and they encouraged a conspiracy of South Vietnamese military officers to overthrow Diem—although Kennedy was shocked when Diem and his brother were assassinated during the coup.

In October 1962, the United States discovered that the U.S.S.R. had planted Soviet intercontinental missiles in Cuba, ninety miles from Florida. A high-flying American "spy plane" provided detailed photographic evidence of the Soviet missile bases. Apparently the Soviets had acted on the request of Cuba's Fidel Castro, who believed that the bases would provide him with security against American efforts to overthrow him. President Kennedy announced a naval blockage of the island to force removal of the missiles. An "eyeball-to-eyeball" confrontation between Kennedy and Khrushchev followed. In a dramatic exchange at the United Nations, American Ambassador Adlai Stevenson displayed the evidence that the Soviet Union had established missile bases in Cuba. Khrushchev "blinked," withdrawing the missiles from Cuba despite Castro's outrage. The Soviet leader was not prepared for the possibility that the crisis might end in nuclear war.

The Cuban Missile Crisis led both Kennedy and Khrushchev to explore ways to reduce tensions. They established a "hot line" link between Washington, D.C., and Moscow. And in the spring of 1963, both world powers and many other nations signed the world's first Test Ban Treaty, which stopped above-ground testing of nuclear weapons.

The President had to deal with serious domestic troubles as well. He tangled with Congress, specifically the wily, autocratic "Judge" Howard Smith of Virginia, chairman of the House Rules Committee. He and his brother Attorney General Robert F. Kennedy fought an ongoing battle with the director of the Federal Bureau of Investigation, J. Edgar Hoover. Attempts to enforce federal court decisions on civil rights in Southern states led to confrontations with the governors of Mississippi and Alabama. Kennedy had to call out the National Guard to enforce federal court decisions mandating that black and white students go to school together. He also forced the leaders of the steel industry to roll back a price increase that, Kennedy declared, would damage the national interest.

The President was looking forward eagerly to the 1964 Presidential election. In November 1963, he traveled to Texas to resolve a dispute that was dividing the Texas Democratic Party. Riding in an open limousine with his wife in Dallas, President Kennedy was shot twice. He died almost immediately. The police arrested a twenty-four-year-old loner, Lee Harvey Oswald, for the murder. Two days later, a local nightclub owner named Jack Ruby shot Oswald dead in full view of television cameras in the basement of Dallas police headquarters. The nation saw its first "live" murder.

The assassination of President Kennedy has been a controversial event ever since, with as many theories as there are students of it. Was there a conspiracy? Were the bullets aimed at someone other than JFK? Kennedy's assassination, the fourth murder of a President in our history, shocked the people of the United States and the rest of the world.

Vice President Lyndon B. Johnson of Texas, who had been in the motorcade in Dallas, was sworn in as President aboard Air Force One. He had been the former Majority Leader of the Senate, a renowned and foxy master of political horsetrading. Some Americans thought that Johnson was crass and vulgar by comparison with the late President. Johnson resented these contrasts. But he was determined to achieve and build on Kennedy's policy objectives, just as President Truman had wanted to carry on FDR's legacy. In his first address to the nation, President Johnson declared: "Let us continue."

Johnson used Kennedy's name as a powerful political weapon, declaring repeatedly, "I'm the only President you've got." He won enactment of many of the measures that Kennedy had not been able to get Congress to adopt—the Civil Rights and Voting Rights Acts, Medicare, the inauguration of the Public Broadcasting System, and programs designed to combat poverty and urban decay and to protect the civil rights of all Americans. In the 1964 Presidential election, Johnson piled up one of the greatest landslides ever, overwhelming the conservative Republican candidate, Senator Barry Goldwater of Arizona.

In the first year of Johnson's full term, the Twenty-Fifth Amendment was ratified. This new constitutional provision set forth rules governing problems of Presidential succession, including disability resulting from illness, as had happened with Presidents Garfield, Cleveland, Wilson, and Eisenhower. It also set forth rules on how to fill a vacancy in the office of Vice President. When a Vice President must assume the Presidency, he, with Congress, can fill vacancies in the line of succession.

Johnson cared profoundly about his domestic programs, but events forced him to become a war President. The Vietnam Conflict was perhaps the most unpopular war in our nation's history. Johnson remembered that such experts as General MacArthur had declared the United States should never fight a land war in Asia. For several weeks, he resisted pressure by his aides to commit American combat forces to Vietman. But he was determined not to let another nation fall to the Communists. He also believed that supporting the new South Vietnamese government had been a major priority of the Kennedy Administration and that it was his responsibility to uphold it as well. In August 1964, an American destroyer was supposedly attacked by North Vietnamese boats in international waters in the Gulf of Tonkin off North Vietnam. Invoking this incident, President Johnson won from Congress the Tonkin Gulf Resolution, a virtual blank check authorizing direct American military action in South Vietnam.

In the Vietnam Conflict, the U.S. Air Force conducted bombing raids on North Vietnamese cities, and more than 500,000 American soldiers served in ground combat. The war tore the United States apart. It was the first televised war. The millions of Americans confronting the brutal realities of combat in their living rooms were horrified by what they saw. Antiwar protests increased in number and passion during the late 1960s. Students protested the draft that would send many of them to fight in an "immoral war." They chanted, "Hey, Hey, LBJ, how many kids have you killed today?" At the end of January 1968—the month of Tet in the Vietnamese religious calendar—Communist forces staged attacks throughout South Vietnam. They attempted to storm the American Embassy in South Vietnam's capital, Saigon. The Tet Offensive was a military failure for the Communist Vietcong, but it showed that American predictions of victory were equally hollow.

In 1968, Senator Eugene McCarthy of Minnesota emerged as a peace candidate in the Democratic Party, and he almost outpolled the Administration ticket in the New Hampshire Democratic primary in February. Several weeks later, President Johnson declared that he would not seek or accept the Democratic nomination.

The campaign for the nomination was marred by tragedy. In April, the great black civil rights leader, Reverend Martin Luther King, Jr., was assassinated in Memphis, Tennessee. Two months later, Robert F. Kennedy, a freshman Senator from New York who was the Democrats' front runner, was shot dead in Los Angeles on the night he had won the California primary. The murders of King and Kennedy deprived the nation of two leaders who could have moderated among the contending factions of American society. The slaying of Kennedy was particularly shocking because his brother John had been murdered only five years earlier. Unrest in the nation's slums and ghettos had plagued the United States in the three years before 1968, and the problem resurfaced that summer as well. Both the Republican convention in Miami, Florida, and the Democratic convention in Chicago, Illinois, were marred by violence by demonstrators and rioters and by the police. A horrified public watched the bloody street battles on television.

The splintered Democratic Party joylessly nominated Vice President Hubert H. Humphrey. He wanted to repudiate President Johnson's Vietnam policy but feared vindictive reprisals by the President. Southern conservatives and right-wing Democrats formed the American Independent Party and nominated Governor George C. Wallace of Alabama. By contrast, the Republicans seemed organized, confident, and moderate. They nominated former Vice President Richard M. Nixon. He seemed to have matured in retirement after losing the Presidential election of 1960 and the gubernatorial election in California in 1962, and he pledged to end the war in Vietnam and "bring us together." In an extraordinarily narrow election, Nixon defeated Humphrey and Wallace; the nation had to wait a day after Election Day to learn the outcome.

President Nixon offered gestures of conciliation, but when he did not act immediately to end the war, protests began anew. Nixon and his aides feared and distrusted domestic dissent. They took stern measures against it, including covert infiltration of antiwar groups by government agents.

In the spring of 1970, President Nixon ordered American forces to carry out "incursions"—raids—into the territory of Cambodia, the neutral nation adjoining South Vietnam. At the end of April 1970, he announced to the nation that Cambodia had agreed to permit these raids because North

KENNEDY, LYNDON JOHNSON, NIXON ——————— 111

Vietnam's forces and materiél were in hiding there. College campuses erupted in protest. Two demonstrations in May led to clashes with state National Guard units that left six students dead at Kent State University, in Ohio, and Jackson State University, in Mississippi. Protests continued throughout Nixon's first term in office.

On July 20, 1969, two American astronauts landed and walked on the Moon, fulfilling President Kennedy's challenge

Richard M. Nixon, the thirty-seventh President (1969–1974), is the only Chief Executive to resign. He was one of the most complex Presidents, and his legacy mixed distinguished achievements—such as his "journey for peace" to the People's Republic of China—with abuses of power, the most famous of which was the Watergate scandal that forced him from office as he faced impeachment. A month after his resignation, he was pardoned by his successor, President Gerald R. Ford, for all offenses he had committed or might have committed during his Presidency.

to the nation in 1961. President Nixon joyfully declared the Apollo XI mission to be the greatest week in the history of the world since Creation. The several Apollo flights confirmed the success and the value of the American space program, but they did not distract the American people from serious problems closer to home.

For most of his political career, Nixon had been known as the fiercest of anti-Communists. Thus, his dramatic overtures to the People's Republic of China and the Soviet Union in 1971 and 1972 were all the more surprising. Many historians have pointed out that only a President with an unwavering anti-Communist record could have undertaken these initiatives successfully. Nonetheless, President Nixon, in fruitful partnership with his National Security Adviser, Dr. Henry Kissinger, demonstrated the imagination and resourcefulness to score notable foreign policy triumphs. Nixon's state visit to China in February 1972, which included face-to-face meetings with Chairman Mao Zedong and Premier Zhou Enlai, won him new accolades as a statesman. The President always was more comfortable dealing with issues of foreign policy than he was in facing domestic issues, and this inclination in turn shaped his Presidency.

President Nixon tangled repeatedly with Congress over economic policy, judicial appointments, and foreign affairs. He insisted that he had inherent Presidential power to impound funds appropriated by Congress. He wrestled with the economy's problems but could find no solution for the twin problems of inflation and recession. He worried about "our political enemies," the prevalence of dissent, and what he and his aides saw as threats to the stability of the government and the national security. He was outraged when a former government official, Daniel Ellsberg, leaked to leading newspapers the Pentagon's secret history of American involvement in the Vietnam Conflict. He was disgusted when the Supreme Court upheld the newspapers' right to publish these "Pentagon Papers." He launched secret government programs to close off any future leaks. Working out of the White House basement, these men, nicknamed "plumbers," monitored dissent as other White House aides prepared an "enemies' list."

Above all, the President worried about the 1972 election. Most observers believed that Nixon would have no trouble winning a second term against even the strongest Democratic challenger. But the President did not feel so confident. Not even Nixon's greatest foreign policy triumph—his reopening of communications between the United States and China—eased his concern. In its efforts to help Nixon secure re-election, the Committee to Re-Elect the President (CREEP) carried out acts of sabotage against Democratic Presidential candidates and spied on Democratic Party officials. A wiretap was placed on the office telephone of the chairman of the Democratic National Committee (DNC). When five officials of CREEP, acting under the supervision of two White House aides, were arrested in the DNC offices in the Watergate apartment complex in Washington, D.C., on June 17, 1972, most people did not notice. It seemed to be only a police-court story, a matter of low comedy. It turned out to be the first act in one of the greatest scandals in American political history.

Nixon was re-elected in a landslide—in part because agents of CREEP had managed to sabotage campaigns of most leading Democratic politicians who had a chance to defeat the President. The Democratic candidate, Senator George McGovern of South Dakota, was a decent and honest man who urged an immediate end to the Vietnam Conflict. But most Americans were persuaded to distrust McGovern because he was "too left-wing." He was able to carry only Massachusetts and the District of Columbia. (During the campaign, Governor George Wallace of Alabama, who had scored impressive victories in several Democratic primaries, was seriously wounded by a gunman in a Maryland shopping center and compelled to withdraw from the race.)

Most Americans soon forgot about the election. They were more interested in the efforts of President Nixon's chief foreign policy adviser, Henry Kissinger, whose negotiations with the North Vietnamese promised to bring an end to American involvement in Vietnam, just as Kissinger's efforts in 1971 had helped to "reopen" China. After one last, brutal series of American bombing raids on North Vietnamese cities at the end of 1972 and at the beginning of 1973, the United States, North Vietnam, South Vietnam, and the Provisional Revolutionary Government or Viet Minh (the organization representing Communist Vietcong guerrillas in South Vietnam) signed agreements that made it possible for the United States to withdraw its combat forces.

While most Americans were paying attention to the last stages of direct American involvement in the Vietnam Conflict, the press, led by the *Washington Post,* had begun to dig into the Watergate break-in. They found a web of corruption and dirty tricks. The more they found, the dirtier and more complex the scandal seemed to be.

In the spring of 1973, the Senate appointed a select committee to investigate Watergate. The committee's hearings soon became a major television event. Even before the committee began its work, the President was forced by public opinion to accept the resignations of Chief of Staff H. R. Haldeman, Domestic Adviser John Ehrlichman, and Attorney General Richard Kleindienst, and to fire a fourth, Presidential Counsel John Dean. The new Attorney General, Elliot Richardson, pledged to appoint a special prosecutor to investigate the Watergate scandal and to back him fully. Archibald Cox, Richardson's former constitutional law professor at Harvard Law School and a Solicitor General under President Kennedy, got the job.

The Senate investigation disclosed that the President had

taped conversations in the Oval Office. Cox demanded that the President turn over the tape recordings to him for use as evidence in the grand jury investigation of Watergate. Nixon resisted. He cited as grounds the doctrine of *executive privilege*—a legal principle protecting the confidentiality of Presidential discussions with aides and advisers. Cox filed suit in the federal district court in Washington for a *subpoena*, or formal court order, directed to the President. Judge John Sirica issued the subpoena. The District of Columbia Court of Appeals upheld Sirica's decision.

The President then proposed a compromise, and his advisers issued veiled threats should Cox refuse to accept the deal. They appealed to Cox's patriotism: The President was dealing with a major war in the Middle East between Israel and Arab states. Cox's efforts, they said, would weaken Nixon's authority. Cox remained firm. He argued that he had a responsibility to uphold the law and that even the President had to bow to the rule of law. The President determined that Cox had to go, but Attorney General Richardson refused to fire him and resigned. Assistant Attorney General William Ruckelshaus also refused to fire Cox and was himself fired, although he tried to resign first. Finally, Solicitor General Robert H. Bork agreed to fire Cox, and he did.

This "Saturday Night Massacre," in October 1973, outraged the nation. The firestorm of criticism prompted the President to reverse his course. In April 1974, the White House staff prepared transcripts of the tape recordings for release to the special prosecutor and the public. But Cox's successor, Leon Jaworski, continued the legal battle for the tapes, and he took the case to the Supreme Court.

On July 24, 1974, the Court unanimously ruled (in an opinion written by Chief Justice Warren E. Burger, a 1969 Nixon appointee) that the President had to turn over the tapes to Judge Sirica. (Only Justice William H. Rehnquist, a 1971 Nixon appointee who had helped to develop the doctrine of executive privilege during his service in the Justice Department, did not participate.) Judge Sirica and Special Prosecutor Jaworski then agreed that the tapes should be made available to the House Judiciary Committee, which had begun hearings on the question of impeaching the President. These hearings became the focus of American public life that summer.

On July 27, 1974, three days after the Supreme Court decision, the committee adopted three articles of impeachment for discussion by the full House. The first article charged the President with obstruction of justice for his role in covering up the activities of CREEP agents in the Watergate scandal. The second accused the President of violating the constitutional rights of American citizens by authorizing secret illegal government investigations. The third focused on the President's refusal to obey subpoenas issued by the committee to obtain documents needed for its investigation.

At the beginning of August, the President released three more transcripts indicating that he had ordered CIA officials to sidetrack and mislead FBI investigations of the Watergate break-in. This "smoking gun" confirmed that there was enough evidence for the House to impeach and the Senate to convict the President on the charge of obstructing justice. Even die-hard supporters of the President in the House and the Senate abandoned his cause. Confronted with the inevitable, Nixon announced that he would resign the Presidency.

Richard Nixon's resignation, on August 9, 1974, marked the end of an era in the history of the Presidency. From the end of the Second World War to the assassination of President John F. Kennedy, the American people had tended to believe that the government was telling them the truth, automatically assuming that the President knew best and that his decisions about policy should not be doubted. The questions raised by

President Kennedy's murder, the public disenchantment with the Vietnam Conflict, and the Watergate scandal shattered public confidence in government. These crises also seemed to indicate that one of the greatest problems facing the nation was an "imperial Presidency" that had to be brought back under control to preserve the Constitution.

CHAPTER ELEVEN

PUTTING THE PRESIDENCY BACK TOGETHER: FORD, CARTER, REAGAN

Nixon's Vice President, Spiro T. Agnew, also had resigned. He had quit in October 1973 when it became clear that he would be indicted for bribery and other charges unrelated to Watergate. The Twenty-Fifth Amendment was used for the first time to deal with the Agnew vacancy.

President Nixon nominated and Congress confirmed the Minority Leader of the House of Representatives, Gerald R. Ford of Michigan, as the new Vice President. When Nixon resigned the Presidency ten months later, Ford succeeded him as President, declaring, "Our long national nightmare is over." President Ford appointed and Congress confirmed Nelson Rockefeller, the former Governor of New York and a perennial Republican Presidential candidate, to the Vice Presidency. For nearly three years—and for the only time in American history—the nation's two highest officeholders were men who had not been elected to their offices.

Gerald R. Ford has been the only President to survive two (unrelated) assassination attempts during his time in office. His two assailants were the first women to attempt to kill a President. Lynette "Squeaky" Fromme was a disciple of the convicted murderer and cult leader Charles Manson. Sara Jane Moore was a follower of another 1970s radical splinter group, the Symbionese Liberation Army. Both Fromme and Moore missed, and the President was unhurt.

In April 1975, two years after the signing of agreements ending American involvement in Vietnam, the South Vietnamese government crumbled in the face of North Vietnamese invasion and Vietcong uprisings. The collapse startled the world by its speed and completeness. At the end of that month, Saigon, the South Vietnamese capital, fell. Television reports showed the last American helicopters taking off from the roof of the U.S. embassy as hundreds of South Vietnamese citizens begged to be evacuated. All the places that had become landmarks for thousands of American soldiers and millions of citizens watching the televised war at home—Da Nang, Hue, Cam Ranh Bay—were now in the hands of the victorious Communists. (Saigon was renamed Ho Chi Minh City to honor the founder of North Vietnam.)

President Ford's great achievement was to restore a measure of faith in the government after the Watergate scandal. He also tried, with less success, to bring inflation under control. But the President outraged many Americans when he granted a pardon in September 1974 to former President Nixon for any offenses against the law that he had committed or might have committed during his years as President.

It became clear that President Ford would not automatically be nominated by the Republicans as their candidate in the 1976 election. Former Governor Ronald Reagan of California mounted a challenge to Ford from the right wing of the party, which Ford barely managed to overcome. The Democrats nominated a political unknown, former Governor Jimmy Carter of Georgia. Carter described himself as a political outsider and promised "a government as decent, compassionate, competent, and full of love as the American people." Carter defeated Ford by a narrow margin. It was the first time in forty-four years that an incumbent had lost a Presidential election.

Jimmy Carter's Administration scored several notable foreign policy achievements. He established formal diplomatic relations with the People's Republic of China. He negotiated a major strategic arms limitation treaty with the Soviet Union. He negotiated and got the Senate to ratify a treaty returning sovereignty over the Panama Canal to Panama at the end of the century. With justifiable satisfaction, the President hailed the Panama Canal treaty as "the most significant advance in political affairs in the Western Hemisphere in this century." He pursued a vigorous policy of pressuring other nations to recognize and expand protections for human rights. And in 1978, with Israeli Prime Minister Menachem Begin and Egyptian President Anwar el-Sadat, he worked out the "Camp David accords," which he hoped would become the foundation for future efforts to achieve peace in the Middle East. On the domestic front, the Carter Administration promoted energy conservation, limited strip mining, adopted stricter ethical standards for government officials, increased federal commitment to protecting the environment, and limited the power and discretion of federal intelligence agencies.

But the Carter Presidency was also a period of frustration and complexity. He and his aides never mastered the delicate task of maintaining good relations with Congress. The Panama Canal treaty offended American conservatives of both parties. The strategic arms limitation treaty was stalled in the Senate and never achieved ratification. The Middle East remained a tinderbox in international politics, despite the President's best efforts, for no other country in the region would join Israel and Egypt in the Camp David accords. The economy's problems continued, defeating the efforts of a third President in a row. The Soviet Union invaded Afghanistan at the end of 1979; Carter's efforts to forge an international trade embargo against the U.S.S.R. failed and drew the outrage of American farmers who depended on grain sales to the Soviet Union. But the problem that eventually cost President Carter a second term was the Iran crisis.

Iran is a significant nation in the Middle East. Its history stretches back more than 2,500 years to the days of the Persian Empire. In the 1950s, the United States had helped to topple Iran's popular, democratically chosen leader, the neutralist Prime Minister Mohammed Mossadegh, and restored the monarch, or *Shah*, to his throne. For nearly thirty years, the Shah ruled with an iron hand, backed by the dreaded secret police, the SAVAK. In the 1960s and 1970s, many Iranian students, some with leftist views and others allied with extremist Muslim clergymen, demonstrated throughout the Western world against the regime of the Shah. Carter, like all other Presidents since Eisenhower, was reluctant to criticize the Shah. American criticism might suggest that the United States would not object to his overthrow. Keeping the Shah on his throne seemed vital to American interests in the Persian Gulf region.

In 1979, protests uniting the radical left, the religious right, and moderate opposition political parties toppled the Shah's regime. An interim government led by a respected moderate, Prime Minister Shapur Bhaktiar, also fell, and the religious right's leader, the Ayatollah Ruhollah Khomeini, flew in from exile in Paris to lead the Iranian "Islamic revolution." The new Prime Minister, Mehdi Bazargan, stepped down in frustration, and the religious faction took over the government of the country.

The Shah was given refuge in the United States. In revenge, a group of fundamentalist Iranian students, with the behind-the-scenes backing of the Iranian government, seized the U.S. embassy in Teheran and took about one hundred hostages, but released nearly half of them. President Carter declared that the United States would never negotiate with terrorists. He also declared that his top priority was the release of the hostages. These two positions left the United States helpless and frustrated.

The Iranians repeatedly captured the attention of the international news media. They staged "media events" with the remaining fifty-three hostages. The hostages' pleas for release and the lobbying of their families with Washington and the news media created the impression that the Carter Administration was powerless to win the hostages' freedom or to punish violations of international law.

The Carter Administration's helplessness was made evident in the spring of 1980 when a military rescue mission ordered by the President dissolved in failure with the deaths of eight American servicemen in a helicopter accident at a desert site in Iran. Secretary of State Cyrus Vance, who had opposed the idea of what many considered a "suicidal" rescue mission in favor of diplomatic negotiations, resigned in protest.

Like his predecessor in the White House, Carter faced a tough challenge for his party's Presidential nomination, but he managed to turn aside the bid of Senator Edward M. Kennedy, the brother of John and Robert Kennedy. Still, the contest within the party hurt the President's chances for re-election.

The front runner for the Republican Presidential nomination, Ronald Reagan, denounced President Carter's handling of the hostage crisis. He promised a return to traditional American values. Reagan won his party's nomination and defeated Carter in a landslide even more lopsided than the Nixon-McGovern race of 1972. The Republican victory was so overwhelming that the party took control of the Senate from the Democrats for the first time in a generation.

During the election campaign, negotiations dragged on between the United States and Iran for the release of the hostages. The Iranians were paying close attention to the Presidential election. They despised Carter and wanted to deny him even the slightest satisfaction. They waited until the moment that President Reagan was sworn into office to release the hostages.

Ronald Reagan, the oldest man ever elected to the Presidency (he was sixty-nine when he took office), argued that most of the nation's economic and domestic problems flowed from the mistaken belief that government could solve these problems. In fact, he declared, government *was* the problem.

Reagan had promised to reduce taxes, balance the budget, and increase defense spending—all at once. Critics declared this set of goals to be impossible and mutually inconsistent. (Even George Bush, who had lost the nomination to Reagan but became his Vice President, had denounced Reagan's policy as "voodoo economics.") But Reagan persevered.

President Reagan almost did not get the chance to govern. Two months after taking office, he was shot by John W. Hinckley, Jr., a mentally disturbed young man. The wound was serious—more serious than the White House disclosed at first—but the President recovered.

More than any other President since Franklin D. Roosevelt, whom he claimed as his hero and model, Reagan used as his favorite political strategy direct appeals to the American people. They welcomed his folksy and candid style. They forgave his habit of making mistakes of fact and law in his speeches and news conferences. But he was one of the most inaccessible of modern Presidents. He held fewer formal news conferences even than Richard Nixon had held in the worst days of the Watergate scandal.

Reagan's first term seemed to be phenomenally successful. He secured the largest peacetime defense buildup in history, as well as a significant tax cut. But these victories carried with them enormous increases in the yearly and cumulative budget deficits. Congress and the American people did not want to make the deep cuts in social programs that the President sought to offset the increase in defense spending.

The budgetary process broke down year after year. Congress abandoned the effort to adopt a compromise budget. Further borrowing and "continuing resolutions" were the tools that Congress had to use to keep the government going. The national debt under President Reagan doubled, as "Reaganomics" turned out to be a poor predictor of how the economy would respond to tax cuts and increases in defense spending. Another indication that the President's economic formula was not succeeding was the "Reagan recession" of 1982.

The President intended his proposed budget cuts to carry out his belief in a severely limited role for the federal government in national life as much as to reduce federal spending. Even where he could not eliminate major government agencies, such as the Departments of Education and Energy, he hampered their work by staffing them with officials hostile to their purposes. But internal fighting among his aides hamstrung the Administration's efforts to articulate and achieve policy goals.

President Reagan's foreign policy was plagued with angry rhetoric and unfulfilled goals. He declared that the Soviet Union was an "evil empire." Not since the period 1917–1933, when the United States did not even recognize the Soviet Union's birth and existence, were U.S.-U.S.S.R. relations so cold. Even so, and although Soviet armies still occupied Afghanistan, President Reagan lifted President Carter's embargo on trading with the Soviet Union.

The President's efforts to bring peace to the Middle East were unavailing. They betrayed a fundamental lack of understanding of the region's problems. Indeed, his approaches to the problems of the disintegrating nation of Lebanon produced some of the greatest disasters of his Administration. He sent a peacekeeping force of American Marines to Lebanon. They were headquartered in an isolated building in the capital city of Beirut. They were targets who could not shoot. A suicidal car-bomb attack demolished the structure, killing 220

Marines and other Americans. A second terrorist attack, on the American embassy, killed more Americans and persuaded the President after eighteen months to withdraw U.S. Marines from Lebanon.

Reagan's greatest concern was the assertion of the Monroe Doctrine in the Western Hemisphere against Communism. He charged that the guerrilla movement in the Central American nation of El Salvador was a Communist conspiracy against a friendly democratic nation, but he ignored human rights violations by El Salvador's government. He denounced the Sandinista regime in Nicaragua as a Communist dictatorship. He declared its opponents, the *contras,* to be the "moral equivalents of our Founding Fathers," despite extensive evidence that the *contras* were corrupt and just as willing to violate human rights as the government. In 1983, the President joined with leaders of Caribbean nations to send military forces to overthrow the Communist-backed government of the 120-square-mile island nation of Grenada in the West Indies.

Reagan won renomination for a second term easily. The Democrats named Walter Mondale of Minnesota, who had been Vice President in the Carter Administration, to oppose Reagan. The Democratic Vice Presidential nominee, Representative Geraldine Ferraro of New York, was the first woman to be part of a major party's national ticket. The Republicans buried the Democrats in a second "Reagan landslide."

Almost immediately, Reagan's new term ran into trouble from many of the same causes that had plagued his first term. Congress had enacted legislation forbidding direct governmental aid to the *contras.* The President's aides decided to evade the law by establishing private channels of privately raised funds. They argued that the Congressional legislation violated the President's inherent power under the Constitution to conduct foreign policy and protect the national security. The secret networks of aid included an elaborate conspiracy to sell weapons at marked-up prices to Iran, then embroiled in the fifth year of a bitter war with its neighbor Iraq. The conspiracy used the profits from the Iran arms deals to aid the *contras*. A second purpose for the Iranian weapons deals was to secure the release of American hostages held by Iranian-backed terrorist groups in Lebanon.

The scandal, which became public in November 1986, prompted another outcry across the land. Investigations and congressional hearings dominated most of 1987—the bicentennial year of the U.S. Constitution—as did the investigations and report of the President's own study group chaired by former Senator John Tower (Republican–Texas). One especially confused issue was whether the President had authorized or approved—or even known about—the diversion of funds to the *contras*. The controversy damaged the President's formerly unparalleled ability to persuade the public to support his policies, crippling his Administration.

Other initiatives failed abruptly, dramatizing Presidential insensitivities and inattentiveness. The most noteworthy was the President's attempt to fill a critical vacancy on the Supreme Court left by the sudden retirement of Justice Lewis F. Powell, Jr., a 1971 Nixon appointee. President Reagan hoped that this appointment would give the conservative bloc on the Court a five-vote majority to overturn many significant decisions long criticized by the right wing, such as *Engel v. Vitale* (the Court had held that required prayer in public schools violates the First Amendment's separation of church and state). In July 1987, President Reagan nominated Judge Robert H. Bork, a scholarly and combative former law professor. Bork's explanations of his views led to his rejection by the Senate by the largest margin ever to turn down a nominee to the Court. Reagan tried again. His second nominee, Judge Douglas H. Ginsburg, suddenly withdrew his name under pressure from Administration officials after confirming news reports that he had smoked marijuana as a student and a law professor. (Ironically, the Administration never had a chance to submit Ginsburg's name formally.) At last, in early 1988, Judge Anthony Kennedy of California, the President's third nominee, was confirmed by the Senate.

The President tried to shore up his Administration by making new overtures to the Soviet Union—moves that were reciprocated by the new Soviet leader, Mikhail Gorbachev. Two summit meetings, one in late 1987 and the second in the spring of 1988, revived the stalled talks between the two superpowers on limiting the growth of their nuclear arsenals.

But whatever benefit the President enjoyed as a result of these summit talks was eroded by the continuing Iran-*contra* investigations and by damaging revelations contained in "kiss-and-tell" memoirs published by key former Presidential aides. For most of his political career, Reagan had frustrated opponents and skeptical journalists alike, for none of their charges or criticisms seemed to "stick" to him. For this reason, he soon won the nickname of "the Teflon President." But the "kiss-and-tell" memoirs managed to cut through the President's Teflon surface. Not only their content, but their mere existence proved damaging to him, for never before in American political history had present or former members of an Administration published memoirs of their White House experiences *before* their President had stepped down.

Former Secretary of State Alexander Haig, former Budget Director David Stockman, former Education Secretary Terrell Bell, former Deputy Chief of Staff Michael Deaver, former Press Secretary Larry Speakes, and former Treasury Secretary and Chief of Staff Donald Regan were sharply criticized for breaching confidences. But these attacks on the moral "sleaziness" of the authors of these books did not obscure the common theme of the accounts—that President Reagan was the single most passive President in the sixty years since Calvin Coolidge (a President for whom Reagan professed deep admiration). The books painted a picture of the President as uninterested in detail, unwilling to give direction to his aides and advisers, comfortable only with a completely scripted day that left him no need or chance to express himself on major issues, and unable to assimilate new information, to comprehend complex issues, or to take charge of his Administration. In fact, Mrs. Reagan, rather than her husband, seemed to be a leading source of political insight and executive decisiveness. As a result, issues of competence, decisiveness, and responsibility seemed likely to play key roles in the 1988 Presidential election.

INTO THE THIRD CENTURY

The 1988 Presidential election took place during the celebrations of the two hundredth anniversaries of the Constitution and the form of government it created. Political observers and historians who compared the quality of our present and potential Presidents with that of George Washington and his Administration in 1789 found much reason for concern and disappointment. The lackluster campaign caused many journalists and citizens to ask: "Isn't there some better way to pick our President?"

Several constitutional scholars, as well as former Presidents Nixon, Ford, and Carter, have proposed that the Constitution be amended to give the President a single, six-year term of office. This idea, they claim, would relieve the President of the burden of constantly worrying about re-election and permit him or her to focus on the nation's needs, hopes, and problems. Opponents of the idea charge that it would deprive the President of the political power that he or she would have as a candidate for re-election; they claim that a six-year President would be a "lame duck" from the moment of the swearing-in ceremony.

Another proposal focusing on the length of the Presidential term calls for repeal of the Twenty-Second Amendment. Ratified in 1951, this Amendment (as we have seen) was in large part a slap at the memory of Franklin D. Roosevelt. The Amendment's critics charge that it is a shameful and partisan attempt to limit the people's right to choose whomever they wish to lead the nation. However, this Amendment, despite its unsavory origins, finds defenders who claim that it has become vital to the Presidency. They argue that a President cannot survive more than two terms of the stresses and strains of the modern Presidency. They maintain that a President who serves more than two terms would thwart the rise of men and women who could succeed him or her in the White House. Would we not run the risk of electing Presidents for life because no alternatives would appear on the horizon until the incumbent dies?

Still another question about the way we choose our President has to do with the ways that our votes are counted. We do not vote directly for Presidential candidates. We vote for *electors*—men and women who cast votes in the Electoral College. To win the Presidency, a successful candidate must amass 270 electoral votes of the 538 available—a bare majority.

If Candidate A gets 50.1 percent of the popular vote in State X and Candidate B gets 49.9 percent, candidate A gets all the electoral votes of State X, and those who voted for Candidate B might as well have stayed home. Thus, it is possible for a candidate to win the popular vote nationwide but lose in the Electoral College, as Grover Cleveland did in 1888. Also, it is possible for an elector to vote for somebody other than the candidate he or she is pledged to vote for. This happens rarely and so far has not affected the outcome of any Presidential election. That could change someday.

Many politicians and scholars have called for an amendment to the Constitution to deal with the problems of the

Electoral College. The most modest amendment would do away with the electors; the electoral votes would be cast automatically once it is known which candidate has won the popular vote in each state. A broader amendment would split each state's electoral vote based on the percentage of the popular vote by the candidates.

The most sweeping and most often proposed amendment would do away with the Electoral College once and for all, replacing it with a system of direct popular vote. Its advocates point to the success of direct popular voting for Senators. Its opponents charge that abolishing the Electoral College would cause Presidential candidates to focus on only those states where the most voters can be found; as a result, states with smaller populations, such as Vermont, Alaska, and Nevada, would be slighted in favor of states such as New York, California, Illinois, and Texas. The argument has not produced an amendment to be sent to the states, nor is it likely to in the years ahead, unless something goes terribly wrong with the Electoral College.

Still other students of the Presidency focus on the powers of the President and whether the office has become too much for one person under our present system. Some say that we should remove some powers and responsibilities from the President—vesting them in the Vice President (to give him or her something important to do) or in Congress or in the Cabinet or elsewhere. Others say that the problem is not Presidential power but lack of power.

Theodore Roosevelt once lamented: "Oh, if I could only be President and Congress together for just ten minutes!" His distant cousin and eventual successor, Franklin D. Roosevelt, observed: "Lincoln was a sad man because he couldn't get it all at once. And nobody can." Several scholars claim that the Constitution's system of checks and balances strangles our Presidents. Therefore, they argue, we must make the Presidency even more powerful. Perhaps the President should have the power to veto only parts of bills that he or she does not like rather than the whole bill. (President Reagan has frequently called for such a "line-item veto" amendment.) Perhaps the Senate's power to approve treaties should be changed so that a simple majority of the Senators can ratify a treaty rather than the two-thirds vote now needed. These and other changes are interesting and often discussed, but no serious proposal has emerged to date.

The problems of electing a President—for how long, how many times, in what way—are fertile sources of ideas to change the Constitution. In fact, such problems plagued the men who created the Presidency in 1787, the ratifying conventions that adopted the Constitution in 1787–1788, and all later students of the Constitutional system.

The American experiment in government had as its most daring feature the creation of a popularly elected Chief Executive. The Presidency is the one political office in which all Americans have a stake and in the filling of which all Americans can have a voice. It is an office of great power and prestige. In the twentieth century, Presidents have assumed the role of identifying the nation's problems and goals and proposing policies to solve those problems and achieve those goals.

But another issue remains unresolved: Now that the Presidency is the "bully pulpit," as Theodore Roosevelt once called it, have the American people come to believe that it is the only office of government with legitimacy and authority? Must we rein in the Presidency? Do we expect too much from our Presidents? Is our ongoing search for Presidential leadership a wild-goose chase that damages our ability to govern ourselves?

These issues are in your hands.

FOR FURTHER READING

(An asterisk indicates that a paperback edition is available.)

The best introduction to the Constitution's principles and history is John Sexton and Nat Brandt, *How Free Are We? What the Constitution Says We Can and Cannot Do* (New York: M. Evans, 1986)*; a more unconventional and very popular treatment is Jerome Agel and Mort Gerberg, *The U.S. Constitution for Everyone* (New York: Perigee/Putnam, 1987)*. An excellent short general history of the United States is Allan Nevins and Henry Steele Commager, *A Pocket History of the United States*, 7th ed. (New York: Pocket Books, 1987)*. The best single-volume constitutional history of the United States is Alfred H. Kelly, Winfred A. Harbison, and Herman Belz, *The American Constitution: Its Origins and Development*, 6th ed. (New York: Norton, 1983). The best study of the Federal Convention of 1787 is Clinton L. Rossiter, *1787: The Grand Convention* (New York: Norton, 1987)*. Richard B. Bernstein with Kym S. Rice, *Are We to Be a Nation? The Making of the Constitution* (Cambridge, Mass.: Harvard University Press, 1987)*, presents an overview of the era of the American Revolution based on the latest scholarship.

There is a mountain of books on the Presidency and on specific Presidents. Some classic studies include: Clinton L. Rossiter, *The American Presidency*, rev. ed. (New York: New American Library, 1960)*; George Reedy, *The Twilight of the Presidency*, rev. ed. (New York: New American Library, 1987); Emmet John Hughes, *The Living Presidency* (Coward McCann, 1973); Richard M. Pious, *The American Presidency* (New York: Basic Books, 1978)*; Thomas M. Cronin, *The State of the Presidency*, rev. ed. (Boston: Little Brown, 1981); and Marcus Cunliffe, *The Presidency* (New York: American Heritage Books, 1986)*. Two valuable collections are Paul Boller, Jr., *Presidential Anecdotes* (New York: Oxford University Press, 1981)* and Paul Boller, Jr., *Presidential Campaigns* (New York: Oxford University Press, 1984)*.

INDEX

Adams, John, 3, 7, 16–21, 30, 69–70
Adams, John Quincy, 28, 29, 30
Adams, Sherman, 102
Afghanistan, Soviet invasion of, 120–121, 124
Agnew, Spiro T., 118
Alien and Sedition Acts (1798), 18–19
Alphabet agencies, 86
"America First" movement, 90
American Independent Party (1968), 110
Anti-Communism, 98, 103, 124, 125
Anti-Federalists, 7
Anti-war movement (1960s), 109, 110, 111
Apollo XI. *See* Space program
Arthur, Chester A., 57–58
Articles of Confederation, 4
Assassinations. *See* President, assassinations
Atlantic Charter, 91–92
Atomic bomb. *See* Nuclear weapons

Ballinger, Richard, 67
Bank of the United States, 32–33
Barbary Pirates, 23
Bay of Pigs invasion, 105
Bazargan, Mehdi, 121
Begin, Menachem, 120
Bell, John, 40
Bell, Terrell, 127
Berlin crisis, 105
Bhaktiar, Shapur, 121
Biddle, Nicholas, 32–33
Blaine, James G., 57, 58
Blair House, 100
Blue eagle. *See* National Recovery Administration
"Bonus Army," 81–82, 101
Booth, John Wilkes, 50, 51
Bork, Robert H., 115, 126
Brains trust, 86
Brandeis, Louis D., 88, 89
Breckinridge, John C., 40
Brinkmanship, 103
Bryan, William Jennings, 61, 62, 66
Bryce, James, 52

Buchanan, James, 39–40, 41, 42, 52
Bull Moose Party. *See* Progressive Party (1912)
Burger, Warren E., 115–116
Burr, Aaron, 20, 24–25, 26
Bush, George, 123

Cabinet, 11, 17, 48
Calhoun, John C., 27, 34–35, 52
Cambodia, 110–111
Cameron, Simon, 48
Camp David accords, 120
Cardozo, Benjamin N., 88
Carter, Jimmy, 119–123
Cass, Lewis, 38, 39
Castro, Fidel, 105, 106
Caucuses, 19–20, 30
Central Intelligence Agency, 98
Cermak, Anton, 85
Chase, Salmon P., 54
Chase, Samuel, 25
Chiang Kai-shek, 100
Chicago Tribune, 100
China, 100, 101, 112, 113
Churchill, Winston S., 91–92, 94
Civil rights, 75, 98–99, 107
Civil Rights Act of 1964, 108
Civil service reform, 56
Civil War, 43–51, 56, 59, 61
Clark, William, 23
Clay, Henry, 27, 29, 30, 35, 37, 39, 52
Cleveland, Grover, 58–60, 108
Clinton, George, 23
Cold War, 98, 102, 105
Colombia, 65
Committee to Re-Elect the President (CREEP), 113
Communist Party, 98. *See also* Anti-Communism
Confederate States of America, 43–50

Congress, Second Continental, 2
Congress, U.S., 7–8, 9, 10, 18, 52–55, 62, 71, 86, 88, 92, 93, 100, 112, 120, 124–125
Conkling, Roscoe, 57, 58
Conservation, 65, 67
Constitution, U.S., 4–7, 22, 43–44
  Article II, 6
  Twelfth Amendment, 23–24
  Eighteenth Amendment, 76
  Nineteenth Amendment, 74
  Twentieth Amendment, 88–89
  Twenty-Second Amendment, 102, 103, 130
  Twenty-Fifth Amendment, 37, 108, 118
Constitutions, state, 3
Contras. *See* Nicaragua
Coolidge, Calvin, 74, 78–79, 127
Corbett, Boston, 51
Court-packing plan, 89–90
Cox, Archibald, 114–115
Cox, James M., 73, 74
Crawford, William, 30
Cuba, 61–62, 105, 106
Cuban missile crisis, 106
Czolgosz, Leon, 63

Daugherty, Harry, 76, 78
Davie, William R., 19
Davis, Henry G., 66
Davis, Jefferson, 43, 44
Davis, John W., 79
Dean, John W., III, 114
Deaver, Michael, 127
Democratic National Committee, 113
Democrats (1824–), 29, 35, 38, 39, 40, 48, 55–56, 58, 61, 62, 68–69, 70, 73, 74, 79, 82, 83, 84, 91, 94, 99, 100, 102, 108, 109, 110, 113–114, 119–120, 122, 125

INDEX 137

Denby, Edwin, 76, 77
Depression of 1893, 59–61
Depression of 1929, 79–82, 84–87
Dewey, Thomas, 94, 99, 100
Dixiecrat Party, 99
Douglas, Stephen A., 40, 41
Dred Scott v. Sandford, 40
Dulles, John Foster, 103

Economy, 35–36, 59–61, 65, 68–69, 70, 78, 79–82, 112, 119, 120, 123–124
Ehrlichman, John, 114
Einstein, Albert, 93
Eisenhower, Dwight D., 81, 102–103, 108, 121
Electoral College, 6, 14, 16, 28, 29–30, 55–56
Ellsberg, Daniel, 112
Ellsworth, Oliver, 19
El Salvador, 125
Emancipation Proclamation, 46–47
Embargo, 25–27
Engel v. Vitale, 126
Executive Mansion. *See* White House
Executive power, 2
Executive privilege, 115–116

Fair Employment Practices Commission, 99
Fall, Albert B., 76–77, 78
Federal Convention, 2–6
Federal Hall (New York City), 8–9
Federal Reserve Board, 70
Federalists (1787–88), 7, 13
Federalists (1789–1816), 13, 16, 17, 18, 19–20, 21, 25, 28
Ferraro, Geraldine, 125
Fillmore, Millard, 38–39
"Fireside chats," 86
First World War, 70–72, 81–82

Forbes, Charles, 77
Ford, Gerald R., 118–120
Fort Sumter, S.C., 43
Fourteen Points, 71–72
France, 13, 17–18, 19, 22–23, 71, 72, 75, 90, 91, 95
Frankfurter, Felix, 86
Free silver, 60–61
Free Soil Party (1848–52), 39
Free trade, 59
Frémont, John C., 39
Fromme, Lynette ("Squeaky"), 118–119

Garfield, James A., 57, 108
Garner, John Nance, 94
George III, 2–3, 6, 7
Germany, 70–72, 90, 91, 92–93, 97, 105
Gerry, Elbridge, 17–18
Ginsburg, Douglas H., 126–127
Goldwater, Barry, 108
Gorbachev, Mikhail, 127
Grant, Ulysses S., 48, 49, 50, 56–57, 91
Great Britain, 2–3, 17, 27, 45–46, 60, 71, 75, 90, 91, 95
Great Depression. *See* Depression of 1929
Grenada, 125
Guiteau, Charles G., 57

Habeas corpus, writ of, 44
Haig, Alexander, 127
Haldeman, H. R., 114
Hamilton, Alexander, 11, 12–13, 14, 15, 16, 17, 19, 20, 21, 22, 24–25, 34, 44
Hancock, Winfield Scott, 56–57
Hanna, Mark, 63
Harding, Warren G., 74, 75–78
Harrison, Benjamin, 59
Harrison, William Henry, 36–37, 59

Hartford Convention, 28
Hay, George, 26
Hayes, Rutherford B., 55–56
Highways, interstate, 103
Hinckley, John W., Jr., 123
Hitler, Adolf, 92–93
Hoover, Herbert C., 75, 76, 79, 80–81, 82, 83, 84, 85, 99
Hoover, J. Edgar, 107
Hoover Commission, 99
House Judiciary Committee, 116
House of Representatives, U.S., 7, 30–31
House Un-American Activities Committee, 103
Houston, Sam, 37–38
Hughes, Charles Evans, 70, 75, 76, 88, 89
Hull, Cordell, 92
Humphrey, Hubert H., 99, 110
"Hundred Days," 86

Impeachment, 6, 25, 53–55, 115–116
Indians, 33–34
Iran, 121–123, 126
  Iranian hostage crisis, 121–123
  Shah, 121–123
Iran-contra scandal, 125–126, 127
Iraq, 126
Italy, 71, 72, 75, 90, 93

Jackson, Andrew, 28, 29, 30, 31–35 (33 illus.), 55
Jackson, Rachel, 31
Japan, 39, 66, 71, 75, 90, 92, 97
Jaworski, Leon, 115–116
Jay, John, 11, 12, 13
Jefferson, Thomas, 11, 12–13, 14, 16, 18, 19, 20, 21–24, 25–26, 34, 39, 44, 104
Johnson, Andrew, 48, 51, 52–55
Johnson, Hiram, 70

Johnson, Lyndon B., 107–111
Joint Committee on the Conduct of the War, 47, 48

Kennedy, Anthony, 127
Kennedy, Edward M., 122
Kennedy, Jacqueline, 104, 107
Kennedy, John F., 104–107, 108, 109, 116, 117
Kennedy, Robert F., 106–107, 109–110
Kentucky Resolutions, 18–19
Khomeini, Ruhollah, 121
Khrushchev, Nikita, 105, 106
King, Rev. Martin Luther, Jr., 109–110
King, Rufus, 28
Kissinger, Henry, 112, 114
Kleindienst, Richard, 114
Knox, Henry, 11
Korea, 101
  North, 101
  South, 101
Korean Conflict, 101–102, 103

Labor, 60
LaFollette, Robert, 79
Laos, 105
Latin America, 65–66, 120, 125
Lawrence, Richard, 33 illus.
League of Nations, 71, 72, 74, 75, 90, 93
Lear, Tobias, 11
Lebanon, 124–125, 126
Lee, Robert E., 49–50
Lend-Lease program, 91–92
Lewis, Meriwether, 23
Lewis and Clark Expedition, 23
Lincoln, Abraham, 38, 40–41, 42–43, 44, 44–51 (47 illus.), 66, 68, 94–95, 131
Lincoln, Mary Todd, 45
Lodge, Henry Cabot, 73

INDEX

Louisiana Purchase, 22–23
Livingston, Robert R., 8–9, 22

MacArthur, Douglas, 81–82, 101
Maclay, William, 9
Madison, Dolley, 27
Madison, James, 4, 10–11, 12–13, 16, 18–19, 25, 26–28, 39
Maine, U.S.S., 61–62
Manhattan Project. *See* Nuclear weapons
Mao Zedong, 100, 112
Marbury, William, 25
Marbury v. Madison, 25
Marshall, John, 17–18, 21, 25, 26, 33, 34
Marshall, Thomas R., 73
McCarthy, Eugene, 109, 110
McCarthy, Joseph R., 103
McClellan, George B., 48–49, 66
McGovern, George, 113
McKinley, William, 52, 61–62, 63, 75
Medicare, 108
Mexican War (1846–48), 38, 39
Mexico, 37–38
Middle East, 115, 120, 124–125
Military-industrial complex, 103
Mondale, Walter, 125
Monroe, James, 22, 28–29
Monroe Doctrine, 29, 60
Moore, Sara Jane, 119
Mossadegh, Mohammed, 121
Mugwumps, *See* Republicans (1856–)
Murray, William Vans, 19
Murrow, Edward R., 91
Mussolini, Benito, 93

Napoleon I, 22–23
National Labor Relations Act, 89
National Recovery Administration (NRA), 86–88

National Republicans (1824), 29
National Security Council (NSC), 98
National Union Party (1864), 48
New Deal, 84, 86–90
New Freedom, 68–69
New Nationalism, 68
Ngo Dinh Diem, 106
Nicaragua, 125. *See also* Iran-contra scandal
  contras, 125–126
  Sandinistas, 125
Nixon, Richard M., 102, 103, 104, 110–111 (111 illus.), 112–117, 119, 123
Nobel Peace Prize, 66, 73
Nuclear weapons
  atomic bomb, 93, 96–97, 98
  limitations, 106, 120, 127
  Manhattan Project, 93, 96, 98

Olney, Richard, 60
Oswald, Lee Harvey, 107

Panama, 65–66, 120
Panama Canal, 65–66, 120
Panic of 1837, 35–36
Parker, Alton B., 66
Parliament, 2–3
Peace Corps, 104–105
Pearl Harbor, Hawaii, 92
Penrose, Boies, 75
Pentagon Papers, 112–113
Perry, Commodore Matthew C., 39
Pickering, John, 25
Pierce, Franklin, 39, 40
Pinchot, Gifford, 65, 67
Pinckney, Charles C., 17–18, 19–20, 26
Plumer, William, 28
Political parties, 12–14, 30. *See also* specific parties
Polk, James K., 37–38, 40

Powell, Lewis F., Jr., 126
President, 1, 44, 64, 129–132
  appointments, 10–11, 48, 126–127
  assassinations, 33 illus., 50–51, 52, 57, 63, 69, 84–85, 107, 118–119, 123
  Commander-in-Chief, 14, 15 illus., 44, 45, 47, 93, 96–97, 108–109
  disability, 60, 73, 93, 94, 103, 108. See also individual Presidents
  election, 6, 19–20, 29–30, 55–56, 93–94, 130–131. See also individual Presidents
  "imperial," 117, 132
  origins, 1–6
  powers, 6, 10, 44, 64, 93, 112–113, 117, 125–126, 131–132
  term of office, 6, 102, 103, 129–130
  two-term tradition, 16, 26, 28, 29, 57, 69, 91, 102
  veto, 2, 6, 32, 37, 58–59, 131–132. See also individual Presidents
Progressive movement, 68
Progressive Party (1912), 67–69
Progressive Party (1924), 79
Progressive Party (1948), 99
Prohibition, 76, 79, 82
Pullman strike, 60

Reagan, Nancy, 128
Reagan, Ronald W., 119, 122, 123–128
Reconstruction, 53, 55, 56
Regan, Donald, 127
Rehnquist, William H., 115–116
Republicans (1790–1824), 13, 14–15, 16, 18, 20, 21, 25, 29, 39
Republicans (1856–   ), 39, 40–41, 52–57, 58, 62–63, 67, 70, 73–74, 75, 79, 82, 84, 91, 94, 99, 102, 104, 108, 110, 113, 119, 122, 125
  Mugwumps, 57
  Stalwarts, 57
Revolution, American, 2–3
Revolution, French, 13
Richardson, Elliot, 115
Rockefeller, Nelson, 118
Roosevelt, Eleanor, 83, 84, 104
Roosevelt, Franklin D., 73, 74, 83, 84–86, 87 illus., 88–95, 104, 108, 128, 130, 131
Roosevelt, Theodore, 62–63, 64–69 (67 illus.), 70, 73, 74, 131, 132
Ross, Edmund, G., 54–55
Ruby, Jack, 107
Ruckelshaus, William, 115
Ruffin, Edmund, 43, 50
Russia, 66, 71. See also Union of Soviet Socialist Republics (U.S.S.R.)
Russo-Japanese War (1905), 66

Sandinistas. See Nicaragua
"Saturday Night Massacre," 115
Schechter Poultry Corp. v. United States, 88
Schrank, John N., 69
Scott, Winfield, 39
Secession, 28, 35, 41, 42
Second World War, 90–97, 116
Senate, U.S., 7, 11, 96, 114, 122, 132
Senate Watergate Committee, 114–115
Seward, William, 48, 50
Sherman, William T., 49
Sirica, John, 115–116
Slavery, 39, 40, 43, 46–47
Smith, Alfred E., 79, 84
Smith, Howard ("Judge"), 106

INDEX

Smithson, James, 30
Smithsonian Institution, 30
Social Security, 89
South Carolina, defies Jackson, 34–35
Soviet Union. *See* Union of Soviet Socialist Republics (U.S.S.R.)
Space program, 103, 105, 111–112
   Apollo XI Moon landing, 111–112
Spain, 61–62
Spanish-American War (1898), 61–62
Speakes, Larry, 127
Specie Circular, 35
Spoils system, 32
Stalin, Joseph, 94, 98
Stalwarts. *See* Republicans (1856–)
Stanton, Edwin M., 48, 50–51, 53
"Steel seizure" case, 101–102
Stevenson, Adlai E. (1835–1914), 60
Stevenson, Adlai E. (1900–1965), 102, 106
Stimson, Henry, 96
Stockman, David, 127
Stock market, 78, 79–80
Stone, Harlan Fiske, 78, 88
Supreme Court, U.S., 10, 11, 12, 25, 33–34, 40, 88, 89–90, 101–102, 103, 112–113, 115–116, 126–127

Taft, William Howard, 66–67, 68, 69, 77
Talleyrand, Charles, Count, 17, 22
Taney, Roger B., 33, 40
Tariffs, 34–35, 59
Taylor, Zachary, 38, 39
Teapot Dome scandal, 76–78
Tecumseh, 36
Tenure of Office Act, 53

Texas, 37–38
Thurmond, J. Strom, 99
Tilden, Samuel J., 55–56
Tonkin Gulf Resolution, 108–109
Tower, John, 126
Tower Commission Report, 126
Treaties, 11, 132
   Ghent (1815), 28
   Guadalupe Hidalgo (1848), 38
   Portsmouth (1905), 66
   Versailles (1919), 72–73, 75, 90
   Test Ban (1963), 106
   Panama Canal (1978), 120
Trist, Nicholas, 38
Truman, Harry S, 94, 95, 96, 97–102, 104, 106–107
Trusts and trust-busting, 65, 66–67
Twain, Mark, 62
Two-term tradition, 16, 26, 28, 29, 57, 91, 130
Tyler, John, 36, 37

Union, 34–35, 41, 43–44
Union of Soviet Socialist Republics (U.S.S.R.), 90, 98, 105, 112, 120–121, 127
United Nations, 93, 97, 106
United States v. Nixon, 115–116

Van Buren, Martin, 35–36, 39
Vance, Cyrus, 122
Van Devanter, Willis, 89–90
Veterans' Bureau scandals, 76
Veto, 2, 6, 32, 37, 58–59, 131–132
Vice President, 6, 16, 19–20, 23–24, 37, 73, 94, 108, 118. *See also individual* Vice Presidents
Vietcong, 109
Vietnam Conflict, 105–106, 108–109, 113, 119
   Tet Offensive, 109
   Tonkin Gulf Incident, 108–109

Virginia Plan, 4–5
Virginia Resolutions, 18–19
Voting Rights Act of 1965, 108

Wallace, George C., 110, 113–114
Wallace, Henry A., 94
War of 1812, 27–28
Washington, George, 1, 4, 5–6, 7, 8–9, 10–16 (15 illus.), 17, 19, 28, 34, 42, 44, 91, 129
Washington Disarmament Conference (1921), 75
Washington Post, 114
Watergate scandal, 113–117
Webster, Daniel, 52
Wheeler, Burton K., 89

Whigs (1828–1852), 35, 36, 37, 38, 39
Whiskey Rebellion, 14, 15 illus.
White, William Allen, 77
White House, 20, 27, 32, 36, 64, 100
Willkie, Wendell, 91
Wilson, Edith Bolling Galt (Mrs. Woodrow), 70, 73
Wilson, James, 5
Wilson, Woodrow, 68–73, 74, 83, 108

XYZ Affair, 17–18

Zangara, Giuseppe, 85
Zhou Enlai, 100, 112

JK
517
.B47
1989

JK
517
.B47

1989